FIX YOURSELF

Lesley,

Thank you so much for your support ♡

Love you

Jill

FIX YOURSELF

THANK YOU FOR FLYING AIR JACK

JILL LIONETTI

MANUSCRIPTS PRESS

COPYRIGHT © 2024 JILL LIONETTI
All rights reserved.

FIX YOURSELF
Thank You for Flying Air Jack

ISBN	979-8-88926-122-3	*Paperback*
	979-8-88926-123-0	*Hardcover*
	979-8-88926-121-6	*Ebook*

Dedication

To all the relationships that have made me stronger

To my friends who have become my family and my support

To my readers who find a piece of themselves in this book and dare to be brave even when broken

To my angels who sent me someone who has opened my heart to trust and love again

Most of all… to my horse Jack… the forever love of my life

Table of Contents

	INTRODUCTION	9
CHAPTER 1:	HORSES ARE THE BEST TEACHERS	15
CHAPTER 2:	LIFE LESSONS COME IN ALL KINDS OF PACKAGES, BUT NONE ARE SENT BY ACCIDENT	29
CHAPTER 3:	SOCIETAL STEREOTYPES—WHO FIXES THE BOO-BOOS?	37
CHAPTER 4:	PARENTS… OH PARENTS… AND FAMILY… OH FAMILY!	45
CHAPTER 5:	LET'S TALK ABOUT SEX, BABY	57
CHAPTER 6:	MEN, MEN…	65
CHAPTER 7:	AND MORE MEN	79
CHAPTER 8:	ALONG CAME A SEX ADDICT	93
CHAPTER 9:	ABUSIVE RELATIONSHIPS	103
CHAPTER 10:	THE FEAR OF BEING MEAN	109
CHAPTER 11:	RAISING CHILDREN	115
CHAPTER 12:	FRIENDS OR FRENEMIES?	125
CHAPTER 13:	WORKPLACE BOUNDARIES	135
CHAPTER 14:	CONFIDENCE AND BOUNDARIES	145
CHAPTER 15:	HUMAN ANIMAL CONNECTION	153
CHAPTER 16:	LOVE YOURSELF AND LOVE UNCONDITIONALLY	161
CHAPTER 17:	THE WORLD IS YOUR OYSTER—LOVE YOURSELF, LOVE YOUR LIFE	167
	ACKNOWLEDGMENTS	175
	NOTES	179

Introduction

Life's timing is a true wonder. As I begin to write this book in June 2023, I am sitting with my mother at her memory care facility, watching her transition to a better place after struggling with Alzheimer's for fifteen years. She created me, and I watched her try to fix everyone throughout her life, make everyone happy, and try to win everyone's love. She had no boundaries, never saying *no*, doing everything to please others with a happy façade while usually feeling miserable and unloved. Yet here she is in her final days, still trying not to let people down… not willing to let go and allow herself peace.

Although I always say I am a rebel and nothing like my mom, I realize, *Oh, but I am*. I have always struggled with boundaries, and the main goal of my relationships has been to keep my partner happy. I had the same goal with my horse. But thanks to my horse, I am now beginning to fix myself and my relationships. What a stage to be set as I begin writing my first book about how I overcame these exact issues to change my life.

I have found that most people believe the more you try to please people, the more they will accept you and love you, thus creating stronger relationships. I have tried to do this in my relationships throughout my life. I have always found it difficult to put myself first or even express my needs.

In my relationships, I have made it a point to understand what made my partner happy and how I could help or fix them, and that became my mission. Many times this involved sacrificing my beliefs and principles while trying to understand someone else's behavior and see things from their point of view while having just about zero boundaries. In addition, my relationships almost always involved people I thought I could help or fix.

Some relationships were abusive, draining my energy as I focused on making sure to please my partner in order to keep our relationship intact. Unfortunately, I continued to feel I was not enough, but they never left until I finally ended the relationship. When I left, I usually felt guilty and still didn't stand up for myself by explaining why I was ending the relationship, but at the time, I am not sure I even knew why.

After over forty years of trying to fix people and make them happy in order to build successful relationships, it took a horse to change my life. His name is Jack.

After years of determination while struggling to figure him out, trying to fix this horse I loved dearly, and almost a year of finally bonding, I learned I couldn't ride him. Ever. Never again. Our last ride—almost a year to the date that Jack, the love of my life, nearly killed me on a trail ride—had been perfection. I suppose it was a gift from my angels. It was like he was reading my mind during that last ride.

After that dreadful trail ride, I had to start at square one with him. I had to put on my big girl pants. I had to grow some huge balls. I had to train this horse *all by myself.* And I did it! I fixed him. But did I? Did I fix *him*? I learned that I wasn't a horrible rider. I also wasn't a wimp anymore. I stood up to him, and in return he respected me. I was ready to have a fabulous year being brave, riding the trails, and enjoying my horse and our newly found trust and understanding. But now I can never ride him again. Was this all for nothing?

No, this was for a much of bigger purpose after all. I have always said Jack came to me for a reason, just like everything does in our lives. The day I learned I could never ride him again, I told my friend that Jack changed my life. He changed my person. Nothing else could have ever taught me these lessons in setting boundaries, standing up for myself, trusting myself, loving myself, and being confident and courageous.

She said, "He has made you a much better horse person for the next horse, and maybe this was a way of saving your life."

And looking back, I realize he truly did save my life in many ways. Yes, I had saved his just by adopting him and paying for life-saving surgery, but his purpose was much more significant. And it hit me like a ton of bricks that day. Jack really was no different than my past relationships, other than the way he could hurt me could physically end my life. That lesson hit the hardest. I didn't fix him. He didn't need to be fixed, just like all the people in my previous challenging relationships didn't need to be fixed. It's up to everyone to fix themselves.

Jack didn't respect me for the first five years of our relationship, and I had to fix myself in order to gain his respect, to fix our relationship, and to survive. Prior to the accident, I had worked with him with a lot of fear and uncertainty and a huge amount of self-doubt. I relied on others, who I was certain knew more than I did. But they didn't know him, and they didn't know more. They just had more confidence and less fear.

By changing the way I interacted with my horse—because he forced me to in order to survive—I learned one of life's most important lessons. Standing up for yourself and creating boundaries is the most important step in creating loving, lasting, and respectful relationships.

Looking back at the past year, I realize how many ways I have changed, and my relationships have changed, and what a better place I am in. And I thanked Jack over and over the day that I learned I couldn't ride him anymore, with tears rolling down my face, and I will thank him every day for the rest of our lives. No human in my life has ever taught me anything close to this. In fact, my mother in many ways taught me the exact opposite.

I realized I could help others improve their relationships and feel better about themselves by sharing my experiences. If you are feeling uncomfortable in your personal or work relationships or feeling like you give a lot more than you get back, this book will definitely touch your soul. Maybe you are like I was, attracting all the energy-sucking people out there who will gladly take you for everything you have to give yet giving nothing much in return. You empathize with them, love the heck out of them, and do your best to make them happy, but in return, what are you left with? Somehow feeling empty, used, and disrespected.

The reality is, without creating boundaries and respecting yourself, you cannot create a respectful, loving, healthy relationship with man nor beast. Every romantic relationship I have been in has followed the same story line, and the same goes for some of my friendships and family relationships. A very well-respected therapist I worked with told me, "Jill, you have the wonderful ability to see the good in everyone and understand why they are who they are and love them for it. But along the way, there are red flags… things that are hurting you, that you just ignore to try and preserve the relationship."

Bingo! And most everyone does this somewhere along the line in their relationships. I took a ten-year break from any romantic relationships in hopes of being able to love myself enough to see those flags.

Everyone wants to be loved and accepted and have long-lasting relationships. Everyone wants people they love to be happy. Many of us feel like we can fix those things we don't like about a person or fix that person as a whole to become a different, happier, "better" person. And a lot of us go too far, sacrificing too much of ourselves along the way, many times ending up in disrespectful and even abusive relationships.

As you read my story, I am positive you will laugh and feel delighted to have found someone who likely makes your relationship blunders seem minimal in comparison. I hope, through sharing my journey and experiences, others can come to transform their lives and love themselves first.

CHAPTER 1

Horses Are the Best Teachers

If you are reading my book, it's most likely you have loved an animal. I have been drawn to animals as far back as my brain will allow me to remember. I wanted to ride horses when I was younger, but my mom wouldn't allow it. She was afraid of them, as she was of most things. Somehow, I turned out opposite of her in a lot of ways, especially this one. She told me never to pet strange dogs, never to go near cats, and she never let me do anything slightly dangerous. Even at amusement parks, she wouldn't let me ride the rollercoasters with my dad.

Despite my mom's fear of animals, I developed a passion for the four-legged furry friends. Now my biggest passion is animals. I massage dogs, horses, you name it… even big barn pigs. I also ride horses, which is considered one of the most dangerous sports in the world. I moved to England right out of college, to a strange country where I knew nobody other than my husband at the time. My mom was horrified and thought I was crazy to do such a thing. I lived in England for nine years, and there my relationship with horses began. I never looked back.

When I think about my early riding days, it was pure naive bliss. These big, gorgeous cuddly horses would carry me around willingly and loyally, despite my lack of knowledge or skill.

In the quaint little city of Durham, in the northeast of England, the first horse I hopped on was a very tall horse named Albert. We were in a large indoor arena, and as usual, the day was a bit dreary. I put on a big old, borrowed helmet and a chest protector, which was required to take lessons in England. I wore some big old rubber wellies, which they said was the thing to wear. Keep in mind, I am afraid of heights.

"*Ooohhh*," I said, "I'm way up here!"

"Yes," said the instructor, who was a young girl. "Now cross your stirrups over the saddle and tie up your reins."

I obliged.

"Trot On!" she instructed the horse.

"Waaaiit," I squealed as the sweet lesson horse slowly trotted along while I bounced all over his back clueless as to what I was doing. I sucked, but I was hooked. From that moment on, I rode every week. We moved to Cardiff followed by Nottingham and then back to Durham, and I rode and rode and rode. I even rode when I was seven months pregnant.

And I was still a terrible rider, but I didn't know. I thought I was invincible. And these horses were tolerant angel lesson horses that knew *exactly* what to do, and they made me look good.

When you believe you're telling a twelve-hundred-pound animal what to do, you feel like superwoman, and it's a huge confidence builder. I rode out in the gorgeous, green, scenic English countryside. I galloped down hills, over stone walls and wrought-iron park benches across the stunning hills and valleys without a fear in the world. Now, I realize I was nothing short of insane.

Horses are amazing creatures. They live in the moment. They do remember the past, but they have no ability to plan the future or plot out mischief. A few excerpts from an article ring very true in my experience and may help with an understanding of these special animals:

"Horses teach us confidence. They are herd animals, and every herd has a leader. If you don't provide the leadership, your horse will."[1] Nothing could be truer. This also gives you tremendous confidence.

"Horses are also gifted at teaching us how to communicate. They don't speak our language, so they base their translations off our body language. They hear our tone and see our actions. Keeping our shoulders back, head tall, and voice strong communicates assertive, but not aggressive, confidence. When a horse is nervous, we can change our body language to eyes shifted down, soft voice, and slow movement."[2] You absolutely *cannot* fool a horse. Your emotions cannot be hidden, which forces you to gain control of your mind and spirit.

"Many adults have a hard time identifying and maintaining their personal boundaries. I mean, haven't we all felt like a doormat from time to time? But our horses show us their boundaries every time we are around them and teach us to communicate ours."[3]

As you read this book, it will become apparent that I basically had *no* boundaries until Jack taught me the importance, necessity, and benefit of having boundaries in my life.

It took me many, many years to truly understand these animals. I started to learn a bit more once I moved back to the states. It took me a while to get back in the swing of things. I found in the US, people rode mostly around in circles in indoor arenas, sometimes outdoor arenas, but it wasn't as gorgeous as the English countryside I was accustomed to.

There seemed to be some snobbery and uppity attitudes from both riders and instructors that took away from the fun and enjoyment of just being with these amazing creatures. I quit for four years until one of my son's friends, who was in fourth grade at the time, said she was going to start riding.

I said, "I am coming with you!"

And so, it all began again when I was about thirty-seven. This is when, unknown to me at the time, I would truly learn to understand these glorious animals and even find a career helping them! That career, being an equine massage therapist, has allowed me to become acutely in touch with their energy, the way they communicate and the pure amazingness of their souls.

I began riding again under an instructor at a local barn. I often rode a horse named Phantom. Other students would look at me in amazement after I rode him, which I found odd as I didn't do anything special.

Then one day a lady said to me, "Has he dumped you yet?"

I said, "No, why would he?"

She said, "Well, he always spooks at the woods and dumps people."

I thought this was odd. He was never fazed by anything in the woods when I rode him. I had no idea then but know now that horses sense a human's thoughts and nervous energy. After he did this, people expected him to do it and became worried by the woods, which caused him worry, and as a result, he spooked! Horses uncover things you may try to hide about yourself. I didn't worry, and as a result, Phantom didn't spook.

After a fun year or so at that barn, we followed our riding instructor to her own home where I began to ride a young four-year-old quarter horse named Hunter. He instantly exposed my poor riding skills. Not being a lesson horse, he expected his rider to tell him what to do. He taught me he wasn't doing anything unless I was confident and positive that I wanted him to do it. I pampered him with a lot of love and treats, and he babysat me like a true friend for fourteen years. We won a lot of blue ribbons flying over little jumps and I adored him.

However, he wasn't immune to emotional trauma I may have been experiencing and was the horse who taught me how my emotions could affect these gorgeous animals. A horrible relationship with a pathological, lying sex addict caused me to doubt myself to the core, and Hunter could feel it. One day I was particularly frazzled while riding him, and he kept hopping around and acting crazy.

Finally, my instructor, who had become a friend in some ways after ten years of riding with her said, "You need to get off. You are making him crazy. He can feel your nervous energy, and it's making him nuts!"

Again, horses uncover things you may be hiding about yourself. You cannot hide your emotions from a horse.

Then… along came the horse that would change my life. I arrived at the barn one day to see a sad looking horse named Wally. "He's a dick," my friend said. "He kicked me and tried to bite me!"

"Hi, buddy," I said to the sad looking gelding.

He looked at me as if to say, "Fuck You! I don't care for people, but… maybe you are okay?"

She had me hold him one day to allow her to groom him and get a picture because she wanted to get some rides on him and sell him. I held his lead line while she brushed and groomed him, and he stood like an angel, just looking at me with his sad, unsure eyes. When she finished, she took the line, and he backed away from her. He could feel her negative energy toward him. She proceeded to beat him with the lead rope and yank the chain down on his nose.

I was furious. He had just stood like an angel for thirty minutes. She said he had no right to back away and needed beaten. I was horrified. He looked extremely scared and unsure. I didn't feel this was the way to treat an animal who really had done nothing other than express his concern. I suggested positive reinforcement for what he did right may be a better approach, and she got super angry. She stated she had worked with horses for years and positive reinforcement was bullshit.

One day a few weeks later she wanted someone to ride him for a sale video. I said I would, which is totally out of character for me. I never ever ride a horse I haven't seen ridden to know how he will behave. Well, something clicked. I loved Wally. He was dreamy to ride and listened to all of my cues with just a light touch.

I loved Hunter more than anything, but he was hard work. She rode him like he was a bicycle. She constantly kicked him and said that was how horses were to be ridden.

"Stop kicking and they stop going," she said.

For me, that was exhausting. Though it wasn't obvious to me at the time, Wally was properly trained and required the lightest touch. However, I loved Hunter and had no intention of buying a horse. I traveled a lot for work and didn't have time nor money to take on the additional expense.

Apparently, Wally had other ideas, and the world knew he needed to be my horse. He proved this by proceeding to poke out his eye in his stall. We never did figure out how he managed this. Saving his eye required nine hundred dollars in vet bills. A couple of months later when his eye was healed, he tripped over a jump, became painfully lame, and could barely walk. The instructor was going to send him to the horse auction.

"*No way!*" I objected. "I will take him! I will pay you for the eye surgery, and he can be mine."

She agreed. Voila! For nine hundred dollars, I owned my first horse.

And that was the day both of our lives changed forever. I found out Wally, formally named Wheres My Wallet, was six years old and had six owners before me. This was not a good sign. I also found out he was a grandson of a famous racehorse named Storm Cat, who is a grandson of Secretariat. Storm Cat has one defining trait… his opinionated attitude.

First things first, he could not be called Wally. I lived in England for nine years, and this means "dumb ass." I began calling him Wally Waffle after a local restaurant, and eventually he became Waffles. He never seemed overly pleased to see me or any humans for that matter, but I was determined to fix him and make him love me.

He hid in the back of his stall and tried to smash me against the wall when I entered. Of course, I got out of the way, and I had no idea that was the worst thing I could ever do with a horse. When you move out of the way for a horse, he instantly determines he is now in charge of you. I moved out of his way for nearly four years.

I had an animal communicator then tell me he hated my voice, and I needed to just silently relay my thoughts, as horses are telepathic. (And, oh, they so are.) She recommended I brush him with a pine tree branch and spray him with sage to clear his aura. She also said I would get rid of him in about eighteen months.

I said, "*Nope!* I am never getting rid of him. I will do all you tell me, and things will all be good."

Well… the fun soon began. I found out he had navicular syndrome, which is an incurable issue horses have with their hooves, but it's manageable. The cause is unknown, and many consider it a death sentence. When you weigh one thousand pounds and your feet hurt, it's not a great thing. Special shoes were recommended, and he tried to kill me when the farrier put them on by rearing up and going backward as soon as the hammer hit his hoof.

"Maybe it's hurting him?" I said.

"No, he's a dick!" the farrier said.

This would be an ongoing theme in many ways with this horse and my life… me not trusting my instincts and what he was telling me but instead trusting other "horse people."

No matter what we did to his feet, he tripped and seemed uncomfortable. He had been Western trained, and we rode English, which resulted in some confusing communication. Something made him decide he should go backward, and I couldn't figure out how to get him to stop. He seemed to find this amusing and just went backward even more.

I finally got over caring about him going backward, and he decided he would spin. He also didn't care to stand at the mounting block, which is what English riders use to get on the horse. I would be patient, and sometimes it would take fifteen minutes or so before I could get on.

My friend decided she would kick him in the chest when he wouldn't stand at the mounting block. Well, one day he decided he wasn't about that. I was getting on at the mounting block, had one foot in the stirrups and one in the air, and he took off galloping and bucking. I managed to sit down, and he torqued me into the air like a small torpedo. I landed confused with a bloody nose.

"Was he bucking?" I asked.

"*Oh, yes!* He was bucking!" my friend said.

"I rode a bucking horse!" I said with delight, just excited to be alive and not hurt.

"He must have seen a piece of hay!" said the five-year-old boy who was riding his horse at the time. I about died laughing.

"Are you going to get rid of him?" everyone asked.

"*No!*" I said. "We will work it out!"

It had always taken me a long time to give up on men who hurt me, but I had never given up on animals. He was going to be my horse for life. *Period. I will fix him.* After all, that's what I tried to do with all the broken men in my life, and he was one of them.

I had a psychic medium reach out to me after almost a year of owning him. He knew my animal massage instructor and mentioned he needed to speak to one of her students. I still am not quite sure how they figured out it was me he needed to speak to. He reached out to inform me that my horse didn't like his name. He didn't want a dog's name. His name was actually John in life, but he wanted to be called Jack.

"Perfect," I said. "I am Jill, and he can now be Jack!"

He told me he was old school and liked to be in charge. I was to be the caretaker and in fact was his soulmate.

Hmmm…this should be interesting, I thought. *I can't let the horse be in charge!*

Jack continued to be a stubborn, pushy horse with a big attitude. I loved him dearly but didn't really trust myself and was a bit afraid of him. The barn I was at wasn't working for us for many reasons, so we left. We landed at a barn where the trainer promised to transform him through natural horsemanship. He had a lot of hay, little turnout, and she wouldn't let me ride him until his brain was right.

As a result of her training methods, he developed a rearing habit while we did groundwork. Having a huge horse stand up on his back legs a few feet away from you is extremely unnerving. He seemed to think it was fun. She told me to make it uncomfortable while he was up there, and then when came down to let him think about what he did.

Well, every time he came down, he looked at me, stuck his tongue out of the side of his mouth, and smirked as if to say, "It's fun watching you almost crap your pants down there!"

This trainer's methods weren't working with Jack, so she decided he wasn't right for her program. She said he possibly was abandoned as a foal. Since she couldn't get through to him, she used the excuse that he must have never been taught the horse ways by his mama.

This was absurd, as his mother is still living, and he has perfect behavior with other horses. That was my last straw. I decided to take him to my friend's house. She had offered for years, but the barn was an hour away with no indoor arena. However, I knew it would be the best for Jack. It turned out it was perfect.

She picked him up, took him to her barn, and walked him out to the pasture. He attempted to rear. She cracked him on the nose with a chain and that was the last time he did that. He felt her confidence, her leadership, and knew she was all business and he'd better listen. At this point he also hadn't taken a step forward with me on his back for months. I could sit on him for an hour… Kick, whip, beg… He wouldn't take a step.

He would just stand and turn his head to my boot as if to say, "Please take your foot out of the stirrup and get off."

At her barn, he slept away his stress in the gorgeous pasture, learned to be a horse, and started to become happy. She ponied him around the trail with the boss horse. This simply means she rode her horse and had Jack follow them while she held him by a lead rope and halter. She rode him and got him to move forward. When I finally rode him, it was like magic. He went forward happily. He walked, trotted, cantered. We went on trails and had a great time. But his feet still hurt after having a horrible farrier ruin them. My friend advised injections might help him feel better.

We went to a leading lameness vet in the area for the injections. Two days later, Jack became lame and could barely walk. The vet advised that he may have had an abscess but refused to visit him.

Ten days later, we rushed Jack to the Ohio State Veterinary Hospital and learned that he had a septic joint. The veterinarians told me the infection may have ruined his joint and surgery may not help him. The surgery was going to cost seven thousand dollars, and they asked if I wanted to proceed. I was hysterical. Of course, I wanted to proceed. I had to save him. I had to fix him.

And that I did. Jack pulled through. It was a long road and took three months until he was able to walk without a limp. When I finally got to ride him again, he didn't want to move forward.

Not this again, I thought.

And that was the day we went on the trail and my life changed forever.

CHAPTER 2

Life Lessons Come in All Kinds of Packages, but None Are Sent by Accident

---

It was a gorgeous day in early May, Mother's Day 2022. I was elated that Jack, my horse, had recovered from his septic joint surgery after eight months of rest and was excited to have a great ride. I hopped on with a positive attitude, knowing horses sense every emotion and don't accept lies. As we began to work in the arena, Jack began his shenanigans, which more or less meant not moving forward… at all. I thought we had gotten past this and began to get frustrated. The stronger he objected, the more my fear factor started to rear its ugly head.

My friend Sonya walked up and said, "Let's go for a trail ride."

This was Jack's favorite thing. He was the best trail horse at the barn the previous year, which was the first year we ever went on a trail ride. I agreed this could be a good idea. In hindsight I realize it was a very bad idea for a number of reasons. Off we went with her horse, Quincy, the barn neurotic, but steady Eddie trail horse.

As soon as we got out of the fenced in property, Quincy started to trot, and Jack took off with great vigor. "Let's switch horses, and you ride Jack! This isn't good," I said. Sonya is a much braver, more confident rider than I am, and Jack would behave for her.

Being slightly bossy and on the opinionated side, she said, "He's an asshole. He doesn't listen to you. You need to ride him or get rid of him! What do you think he is going to do? He won't run ahead of Quincy!"

I had been boarding at Sonya's barn for just over a year. Jack wasn't listening to much I had to say when I first arrived, and our relationship had been rocky as always. Sonya has a kill or be killed mentality and had mentioned a couple times that I am not "tough" enough for Jack and his opinionated, somewhat unforgiving personality.

I could feel my heart nervously racing. Now feeling like a wimp, I squeaked out "Umm… maybe buck me off?"

She said, *"Let's go!"*

My nonobjecting, people pleasing, unconfident self-obliged. As in all past relationships, I never trust myself or my instincts.

Nor do I stay true to myself. I figure the other person knows better, or I just choose to do what will make them happy. Off we went. Jack took the lead at the trail entrance since Quincy became his neurotic self and refused to enter the trail.

Quincy worries all the time about everything. He hates raindrops, flies, and anything that tickles his fancy that day. Today he was worried about entering the trail. Jack led the way like a star. We saw a bunch of deer. He nicely said hello and took charge of taking care of me. Happy day!

A feeling of peace and relaxation came over me. All was going well. Until, not knowing the trail well, I took a wrong turn. No big deal, though, as we came to an open area we could use to circle back to Quincy.

"Sorry, Jack," I said as we started to turn back.

At that moment, he realized Quincy was now in the lead and headed off like a roaring bucking bronc! Panic rushed over me, but I tried to remain calm and in control.

I heard myself squealing all kinds of things like: *"Oh, Sonya! See, I told you… Whoa, Jack. Whoa!"*

As we reached Quincy, he slowed down and I thought, *Praise God…*

But no… he kept bucking, and I could feel the saddle smacking my ass like I was on a bucking bull! Off I went, over his shoulder! Things were blurry, I could hear hooves by my head and felt panicked that I might get stepped on. I tried to crawl but face-planted. Finally, my head became clear, I spat dirt out of my teeth, and I managed to stand up. Then felt a sharp pain under my boob. I was alone. I saw Sonya off in the distance leaving.

What the hell? She left me?

"Hey did you fall off, too? My boob is broken!"

She continued walking, unfazed by my comment. I was certain I had bruised or broken ribs as I couldn't laugh or cough or breathe too deeply for a couple of months without feeling like I was being stabbed!

She shouted back, "You are breathing, and your limbs are moving, so I am going to find the horses!"

Okay, I need to follow her, or I will be lost in the woods, I thought. Then I started running after her as I had no idea how to get out of the trail.

"You know you have to lunge him now and get back on. Right? I thought that wasn't going to end well. You looked like a bronc rider," she said.

Holy hell, I thought. Sonya never has said anything even bucked, which made me realize these must have been really big bucks! I was alive. I was barely hurt. My angels were definitely watching over me, and this was definitely some kind of lesson. *What am I going to do?*

We got back to the barn, and there were the horses. Of course, they found their way back. Jack was happily eating grass as if nothing ever happened, and then he saw me… His eyes widened. "*Oops!*" came over his face.

I got the lunge line, a long line used to exercise the horse. One end is attached to the horse's halter, and the person holds the other end and directs the horse to move around in a circle at a variety of speeds. Adrenaline took over for me, which often happens after I get hurt… bravery.

As soon as I asked him to move forward, we were off to the races. He sensed that I had some balls at that moment, which was rare for me. I was attached to a twelve-hundred-pound kite that was trying to cow kick me every chance he got. A cow kick is a back leg being thrown out to the horse's side in an effort to kill the human!

Out of breath, ribs killing me… we went and we went until he finally listened, calmed down, and did what I was asking. And now it was time to get on…

He stood at the mounting block like a perfect gentleman—*not* usual either—and then walked off with a slight nudge. *It's all me,* I thought. *He knows I'm a doormat.* Because all I had done for five years was try to make him happy, try to do what he wanted, he had taken charge. I had trained him how to treat me, just like I do with everyone. He had been trying to tell me for years I needed to be a stronger person. He was sent to teach me the lesson I needed most. "Stand up for yourself, Mom! I love you, so don't make me kill you!"

Jack and I... it's definitely been a ride. Before I owned Jack, I had ridden horses, and that's about it. I didn't understand their brains, their health, or anything else. Little did I know that Jack was here to teach me not only about horses but more about myself than I ever could imagine. I had been through a series of romantic relationships where I never set boundaries. I soon learned he was here to teach me one of the most valuable lessons I have ever learned.

After that day on the trail, my life began to dramatically change forever. My life had been a series of lessons I had failed to pass. Parents, relatives, friends, men, dogs... they all hurt me. But a horse... well... he could kill me. I *had* to do something about it... Me, all by myself. Though I had thought about taking him to a trainer, I knew this wasn't about him. This was about me. I need to start at square one, back to basics. He was going to respect me, no matter what it took.

Little did I know this was all in my control, and it didn't take much at all. When you watch horses in the pasture, there is always a leader. That leader has hard physical boundaries and doesn't allow any other horse to do anything he or she doesn't find acceptable. That leader makes sure all the horses are doing what keeps the herd safe. And guess what? All the horses follow that horse, listen to that horse, and look to that horse for guidance, *no questions asked*. Why? Because horses crave leadership and confidence.

They don't want to follow an unconfident wimp that could lead them to their death. Neither do people. A horse will take every inch from you that you give. If you take one step back when he comes at you, you lose. He is now in charge. He requires an actual *physical* boundary to respect you. He can't take a step to get a cuddle unless you ask him.

Enforcing these boundaries with Jack was painfully hard for me. Afterall, I wanted cuddles and I wanted him to love me. But guess what? He still loved me and he followed me *more* and finally respected me once I was clear with my expectations and set my boundaries.

The horse trainer that changed my relationship with my horse, Carson James, guided me on this journey and said something that resonated well. He reminded me that just when the horse is about to do what is being asked, people lose confidence and give up. And isn't that true across the board in life? People try for a while and when something doesn't work quickly enough or gets too hard, they give up, lose confidence, and don't want to fail.

This was like magic with my horse. Because when you ask, and give up, the horse thinks the thing he is doing is the right answer. He is doing what he thinks you want and what is easy. When you hang in there until he gets the right answer, he easily learns what is expected.

Animals provide us with a great way to understand ourselves because they are a reflection of us. Once I stood my ground, set the rules, and became a confident leader, this horse would go to the moon and back for me. He wasn't going anywhere when I was a wimp either because who would walk away from treats and pets and everything good? Not this horse and not any human. But he didn't respect me, and he would hurt me because he could. Because I set that standard that it was okay. All that time I tried my best to fix him, but the moment I fixed myself, it was like magic… he was the perfect horse.

This translated into all other aspects of my life. My relationships with friends, family and bosses began to change for the better. I was able to say *no* more and stand up for my beliefs and what was important to me, just like I had to do with Jack. In return, nobody stopped liking me or being my friend, but instead they actually respected me more and our relationships became more open and honest.

I wasn't unlike most people, who believe the more you do for someone, care for someone, give them what they want and make them happy, the more they will love you and the longer they will stay around. And they may, but this will not be the healthy, loving, and respectful relationship we all need and deserve. We can still love, care, and give of ourselves while at the same time creating healthy boundaries and honoring ourselves, which in return will result in a more respectful, healthy relationship.

All creatures big and small cross our path for a reason, or to teach us a lesson, which may just change our life.

CHAPTER 3

Societal Stereotypes— Who Fixes All the Boo-Boos?

Many people believe that making your partner happy will build a strong relationship and possibly fix their pains. Although times may be changing, the general stereotype of our society is that women fix all the boo-boos and make everyone happy. I, like many of you, grew up watching my mom put on a happy face to please everyone, fix everyone's boo-boos, and make everyone happy. Yet all the while she was making herself miserable. She didn't stand up for herself or create any boundaries, for fear of being rejected.

Growing up, everyone said my mom was the most fun and always cheerful. She let us do whatever we wanted. I had no curfew. When I was fifteen, my friends would come over with a bottle of booze, and we would drink. She wanted us to like her. My friends did, but I really didn't.

At home she was judgmental and always telling me I wasn't good enough. I had to be prettier, smarter, and better than all the other girls. I had to fit her perfect picture. But I didn't want to. She had forced herself to fit into that pretty picture her whole life. She wanted me to fit into that same picture so people would love our family picture, the perfect picture she always desired.

In fact, she was voted the prettiest, most popular, and all that jazz in high school but still had a huge inferiority complex, believing she wasn't good enough, liked enough, or accepted enough. She made my dad dinner every night, took care of the house, went to many business dinners, and was beautiful eye candy… all in an effort to get the kind of love she wanted from him and approval from everyone. But she never thought he really loved her.

She never trusted him or anyone else. She always felt people were saying negative things about her, thinking negative things about her. The reality is he did love her. It just wasn't the perfect picture she thought love should be. She craved acceptance. Don't we all?

Looking back, I suppose the lessons learned from my mother taught me more about how to make other people happy than how to value and respect myself and my own happiness. Unfortunately, I took this approach with my own children. My heart just wanted them to be happy, resulting in me being a poor disciplinarian. I hated to see them fall, fail, or cry. I did my best to make sure they didn't, which didn't set them up for success and didn't earn me much respect as a single mother. In later years, lessons were sent my way in the form of romantic interests and pets, and I was always determined to fix them. I kept repeating the mistake and doing the same thing over and over again. Insanity… yes?

It's been pretty much the same thing with my animals. My dogs always love me to bits, but they aren't the best listeners because of my poor disciplinary skills and lack of boundaries. The dog I spent three years trying to fix, Kuro, was different. He listened to me because I learned to be a disciplinarian to try and fix him.

My son brought him home in 2012 from the rescue he worked at because he was going to die. He was a frail, extremely scared Malinois, pitty mix. We bonded instantly. Fearful dogs usually have one of two responses… flight or fight. At first, he chose flight. Then he grew to be a scary ninety-pound, extremely strong dog, and he decided instead of fleeing, he would fight. He bit someone, and I felt I better hire a dog trainer.

She recommended a dog behaviorist because of the severity of his fearful and anxious behavior. I clicker trained him, and he was the perfect boy because of my dedication to fixing him. I never had visitors and was a bit of a hermit because everyone was extremely afraid of him. Then one morning, for no reason at all, he bit my arm. The bite of a Malinois is one of the strongest animal bites, second only to the hyena.

I was horrified, and he seemed to not even know he did anything. The unpredictable behavior continued. For only one hour every morning after he ate, he maybe would decide to bite me for no reason. I did everything possible to try and avoid this and try to fix this behavior. He was also on medication for anxiety. The last time he bit me was horrifying. I also knew he was a danger to my other son. He originally cowered from him, but as he became fear aggressive, he would choose to go after him and cornered him a couple of times. He just wasn't a happy animal, and life wasn't fair for him. He was troubled.

The behaviorist and trainer said, "Jill, you are the perfect student and have done everything right. Some dogs, like people, have mental issues. Because there is no trigger, we can't really help you or tell you what to do."

"Oh, my god, I am going to have to put him down. Aren't I?" I cried in despair.

"We can't tell you what to do, but we have no further way of helping you."

I had no choice other than to put him down. That dog broke my heart in a thousand pieces and took a piece of my soul. *Surely I can ditch the rotten men now,* I thought! I was wrong…

My romantic relationships all lasted until I ended them. I ended them after years of trying to see things from my partner's point of view, accept things I didn't agree with, and hope to fix them. But they were all the wrong things for *me*, and I would give and give and give to make my partner happy.

Did I fix them? *No.* I always felt a bit empty and not good enough. I never said *no.* I sacrificed my needs and values. But they stayed around. Were they healthy relationships? *No!*

Was I respected? *No!* Was I *loved*? Well of course! It's hard to not love and stay around someone who grants all your wishes.

I can see in hindsight many of the takers I have enabled through the years. One friend in particular spent every visit, while she was supposed to be giving me riding lessons, complaining about *everything* in her life. She talked about the same stories over and over. I tried to help her, felt bad for her, and wanted to help her be happy with her life, but she never changed a thing. And she rarely asked about me, my life, or how I was doing.

I didn't agree with the way she treated animals but continually bit my tongue to keep the peace. And finally, when I got my own horse, that became too much. I left with my horse but tried to keep things on good terms. Rather than saying what I really felt, I tried not to hurt her feelings. Well, in turn, she blocked me and never allowed me to see the horse I rode for fourteen years again. That's how far trying not to hurt someone's feelings got me. I am learning slowly.

In my professional life, it's much of the same. I have been in technology sales for the majority of my career. At work, I was always successful, but never really respected. I always felt like something was missing. I was a top seller but not the star. I was never the person everyone called for advice. Why? People follow and respect people who exude self-confidence and demand respect.

However, I sure was good at keeping my boss happy. One boss was so patronizing and down-talking to me that some colleagues mentioned it to me after a team call. I never told him how I really felt about this unfair treatment that the men on our team never experienced. I didn't stand up for myself. And when the opportunity for a promotion came along, I didn't get it. The person who stood up to him the most did.

Does this enabling, fixing, making others happy create a happy, healthy respectful, strong relationship? *No.* I spoke with Dr. William Bixler who specializes in treating sexual addiction and works with addicts, their partners, and family members. He is a Certified Sex Addiction Therapist (CSAT), having received training from Dr. Patrick Carnes, one of the foremost experts on sex addiction treatment in the US. He has been engaged in clinical practice in a variety of mental health settings since 1978.

He said, "The fixers end up feeling a tremendous burden and even guilty for not being able to fix their partner or being able to walk away."

And, yes, I always feel bad for ending the relationship. I never actually dismiss my exes from my life. They *all* still reach out for a variety of reasons. I let them because I don't want to hurt their feelings.

I had a friend once tell me, "Jill, you train your partner how to treat you. What you allow will continue. If you don't like it, don't allow it."

But I always have that fear that they will just leave and find someone else who does allow it. Why would that be so bad anyway? I have never found out because I have never stood up for myself and asked for what I needed in the relationship.

A few chapters will be dedicated to these stories and likely will make you all feel much better about yourselves when you hear the crazy things I have tolerated!

I'm still learning, but I know we all feel the need for acceptance—many times to make relationships successful, many times at a large cost to our own self-worth. Yes, we all must make compromises and consideration for our partners' needs, but don't forget your own along the way! Happiness comes from within. If you rely on someone else to create your happiness, you will be on an endless quest. You cannot fix everyone else's boo-boos. The only one you can actually fix is *you*!

CHAPTER 4

Parents... Oh Parents... and Family... Oh Family!

"Children begin by loving their parents; as they grow older they judge them; sometimes they forgive them."

—OSCAR WILDE

The truth be told, that is exactly how it goes. As a young child, you believe your parents are all-knowing and that the way they live and treat you is the same for all parents. You love them and are completely oblivious to how much their actions and treatment will form the person you one day become. When you become a parent, you realize there is no rule book and you have no clue what the hell you are doing. But you do know how much you love your child.

When do we begin judging our parents? I think it begins as teenagers when we think we know everything, but in adulthood, the reflection becomes much different. For me, there has been a lot of judgment… and forgiving. I think I have landed at the point of forgiving. As for family, well you don't pick 'em. You just get plopped into a way of life that surely will form yours.

I have the memory of an elephant, and it's photographic, therefore I have a pretty clear picture of my life since about the age of three. I can tell you that as far back as I can remember, I liked boys. I wanted to kiss cute boys, have boyfriends, and have boys like me. I never thought much of it until once I was suddenly reflecting on my awful selection of partners.

While sitting chatting with my therapist, who is extremely well-accomplished in her field, I said, "I think maybe I was abused as a very young child."

"Why do you think that?" she said.

"Well, I have loved boys since nursery school. Always wanted to have a boyfriend and to kiss them… but I always *hated* men."

Even when shoe shopping, I would *never* allow the man, Jim, to come near me. Only the lady, Martha, was allowed to measure my feet. I hated all my uncles except two. Oddly enough, both of those uncles were bad boys, which I couldn't have possibly known at the time, but they fit the type of men I would have relationships with later in life. They were fun, always laughing, and crazy. My dad was never any of those things. I didn't want men anywhere near me. It all just seemed odd.

"I just have a weird feeling for some reason," I told her.

She shared with me that usually at that age, children don't really grasp the romantic connection. I was either very ahead of my time, or something happened to make me realize this.

"Do you want to know?" she asked.

"Not really," I said. "I just feel like I know it happened, but it's done now so no point in knowing."

Oddly enough, this all came up when I least expected it while chatting with a medium about my horse. I have a big interest in clairvoyance, psychics, mediums and the like. I earlier mentioned this medium, who had reached out about my horse's name. In the beginning of a session, he said he had something to ask me but wanted to wait till we had spoken a while because it was sensitive. He then asked me near the end of the session if I knew I had been abused as a child around the age of two. I about fell out of my chair. He described the person, and I realized who it must have been. I sent him a picture, and he confirmed that was indeed the person. I will spare you the details. He said it didn't affect my life because I was very young. But maybe it did?

I never brought this up with my parents. We didn't really have the kind of relationship where we spoke about anything serious. My dad didn't speak much at all, and my mom just skirted around issues. My parents never really conversed with each other or us much at all—no real conversations ever about anything real or important. I assume they were raised that same way.

My dad's parents came over on the boat from Italy and spoke no English. My mom's parents just seemed fun, but I am pretty sure her father was a somewhat abusive alcoholic. Who can blame them for continuing along similar paths as their parents? No heart to heart, emotional conversations really happened in our family.

My dad was *never* around because he worked from sun up to sun down, and when he was home, he didn't really speak to anyone—not us, not my friends, and not my mom. He ate, read the paper, watched TV and snored.

When I was in fourth grade, my parents were separated for a while. It didn't change much about my relationship with him. In fact, I think I saw him more because he would take us for car rides every Sunday. He never talked. He just played music in the car and took us to see our grandparents. It didn't bother me at all because I just thought that's how all dads behaved, and I loved him regardless.

My friends were afraid of him. The only time he really interacted with us was our Christmas party every year. He was the bartender and made me Shirley Temples. He laughed and had fun… not really with me but with the people there. I loved that. And that was the only real time I ever would see him have fun.

At other family holidays, he would talk to the men or older boys, mostly about car business, which was what he did for a living. If I tried to chime in, I was pretty much ignored. I loved him, didn't judge him at all, and pretty much thought all dads were the same way. Yeah… I'm pretty sure that affected my life and my relationships in a big way.

First, let's talk about daughters with no real father figure. According to Ryan Light at Beat Anxiety, "Fatherless daughters may struggle with trust issues, fearing abandonment or rejection."[1] This can cause the need to seek validation and acceptance, relying on others for self-worth making them vulnerable to unhealthy relationships and codependency.

Hello, me! Back then, I thought most dads were just the way my dad was… never around, not talkative. When I was in grade school, I had a couple friends with dads who were fun and friendly, talked to me, and played games with us. *I loved them! Superdads!* They made me feel special and loved. I wanted to be around them and was always excited when they would come home.

My dad worked and didn't do any activities with us. I don't judge him for that today. He worked to provide for us, which is what he felt he needed to do. And now I know he is OCD and oh so many things I never knew because he was a total stranger to me. I only really got to know him in the last ten years since he retired to care for my mom and especially when he became ill and I had to care for them both.

Then there was my mom. Her main concern was what other people thought. Hence, her children needed to be perfect. The smartest, the prettiest, the best dressed, the best grades, and on and on and on we could go. I got a nose job when I was fourteen at her suggestion because my nose was too big and not perfect.

She also had to be perfect. She used to cry when she came home from the hairdresser because he did a poor job. She would try on loads of outfits before going out and always asked me if her butt looked big. She *never* went out of the house unless she looked like Miss America. And she had me as her child, who couldn't be more opposite of these things.

I liked to play in the dirt. I liked to play kick the can with the boys, riding bikes and skateboards. I liked to wear bell bottom jeans and T-shirts. She made me get weird haircuts and wear dresses and told me to never pet strange dogs and to stay away from cats. I talked to every animal I saw… Today I am a certified animal massage therapist and spend most of my free time with animals! I usually dress in barn clothes or sweats, hate to dress up, and I wear minimal makeup. I would say I am nothing like my mom… but maybe I am?

She always wanted to make everyone happy and have everyone like her. As I mentioned earlier, I had no curfew. I could have friends over drinking, boys over in my room or in the basement. I could go to a concert, have a hang-over and not have to go to school the next day. No rules. She flirted with my boyfriends like it was her job. I found out later in life that many of them dreamed about having sex with her. *Lord ew!*

I like to think I don't care who likes me or what people think about me. However, as I embarked upon writing this book,

I realized I have fallen into that rut in most relationships. I don't care about what strangers think like she did, but I certainly do care about people I am close to. And maybe I try not to care about what people think because I tried not to care about what my mom thought. She would regularly tell me, likely without realizing it, that I wasn't good enough.

"Why did you get a B?"

I was more or less a straight-A student. The photographic memory served me well.

"I got a B because a B is good and its above average, Mom," I would say with the attitude I had toward her twenty-four-seven.

"Well, it's not above average for you!"

By the way, I was the class valedictorian—a thing my dad never knew until he was eighty-eight and a friend of mine told him.

"If you keep eating like that, you will be two-ton Tessie."

Meanwhile I had the body all of the girls wanted.

"You need your head examined."

Around the age of fourteen, I was nominated by a local department store to model their clothing. I was very thrilled and excited! "You can't be a model! Your boobs are too big!" my mom told me.

Whew… shattered my dreams of being a runway model forever. Now this one I need to explain a tad. I started to develop boobs at the young age of eleven, and by the age of twelve they were sizeable, which was young back in my day. The boys were obsessed. They would try to grab them at recess, and they were the main topic of discussion always.

They grew to DD, bigger than anyone else's, and this remained the number-one focal point of my life. In high school on spring break, the guys actually offered me two hundred dollars to enter a wet T-shirt contest just so they could see them! *No way* was I doing that! My dad made me button my shirts to the top to hide them. As a result, I was super self-conscious when every other girl on earth would have died for my big boobs.

According to the therapist I saw later in life, this boob comment was likely my bull's-eye, meaning a life-defining moment. I didn't think so at the time, but I certainly have never forgotten it, and I was always extremely self-conscious of them!

My mom always had some kind of envy toward me, chip on her shoulder, or feeling of being inferior or not liked. She hated to be left out of conversation, especially if people were laughing. She always assumed they were laughing at her. I was very close to her mother and her sister. They were two of my favorite people on earth. They were so fun, they laughed, they were crazy, and they made me smile. She was always worried about what people thought, or about me getting hurt, or really anything she could muster up the energy to worry about. She hated that I was close with them. Her longing to be accepted and liked the *most* was very apparent all through my childhood.

Her sister also likely had a huge impact on my view of relationships. I looked up to her and thought she was amazing! She was one of my very favorite people. Her husband, who became her ex-husband when I was a teenager, was one of the few men I liked in my family. Of course, he was one of the wild ones. He always cheated on her and had other women. But he came in and out of her life, and they would be together and apart off and on most of their lives. That example set me up for another atrocious example of what a relationship should be like and what women should tolerate.

Clearly, I didn't have great examples of what relationships or marriages should look like. After being married for nine years, I left my husband in England and moved back to the US. He simply wasn't a part of our lives. He played and coached professional hockey. His life revolved around just him from a young age, and it was the same while we were married.

I tolerated it when it was just me and him, but when he didn't get involved in the lives of our children, broke promises to them, and just lived his life, I'd had enough. I had to move in with my parents for almost a year. I got a crappy job selling copiers and worked my tail off. My mother always criticized my parenting.

She also felt I should spend all of my nonworking time with my kids. When I went out with friends, she was furious. She called me a slut and asked me if I got divorced to just have fun. "No, Mom… I got divorced because I didn't love my husband and wasn't going to lead a miserable life forever."

She said, "Well, I couldn't have afforded to get divorced."

I angrily replied, "Well, you could have if you'd gotten a job and didn't just bake lemon bars and cookies and go to junior league!"

When I was growing up all she did was complain about my dad. At one point they were separated. He came back when her father passed away. Interestingly enough, when I moved back home with my kids, he asked me, "Are you sure you are doing the right thing? Have you thought about your little gumpers?" Meaning my boys.

"Yes, Dad. But in the end, they will grow up, and I will be left with someone I don't love. Is that why you stayed with mom?"

"Yes," he said.

Relationships… what a complicated web.

My dad was nearly a stranger, and my mom and I never got along. My mother was always worried I didn't like her. We had nothing in common. She loved to shop, worried about everything, and was very much into material things. Nothing like me but, then again, we both have that common need to make others happy, to fix them, and to be accepted.

When my dad retired at the age of eighty to care for my mom who had Alzheimer's, I then started to realize the reality of their relationship. He actually lived through a terrible flu, double necrotic pneumonia, sepsis, and MRSA at the age of eighty-six simply because of his purpose to care for my mom. He asked about her every single day for four weeks of being in the ICU and almost not making it out alive. Then he lived through COVID at the age of eighty-nine for the same reason.

He refused to get much help caring for her but slowly realized he needed it. He was obsessive and controlling. Everything needed to be perfect with her—the house, her hair, her outfits… everything. He never wanted her to move or touch anything. He combed her hair all the time. He actually had a comb in his pocket to be sure she looked perfect. Yes, it was very kind and endearing but also exhibited some of his OCD because she started to hate it in her final phases of the illness.

Throughout their relationship, she had always been painfully insecure, always trying to please him, and never feeling good enough for him or anyone else. They never really talked or showed much affection. And that was what I thought married people's lives were like. I finally started to get a glimpse of why she had a large amount of animosity toward him throughout my childhood.

I had always thought she was the nag, pushing him away, but now I saw both sides of the story when I had to care for them while he was ill. I saw how controlling he could be and how concerned he was about how she looked and behaved. He also tried to control me. In the last year, after my experience with my horse, I was able to stand up for both myself and my mom and tell him what he needed to hear. Thank you again, Jack.

But all of this, yes, it formed who I am. I don't blame them. I feel you can't blame parents for who you are after a certain age. You become an adult, see the world, create your values, and live your life. You own it. You are responsible for you. Yes, it contributed to my need to be accepted, always have a boyfriend, keep him very happy, be an enabler, be codependent, and never put myself first, but I made those choices. And each one made me stronger.

Thanks, Mom. Thanks, Dad. And yes, I did judge them for a while. But then I remembered… we parents, we have no real idea what we are doing because, after all, there is no rule book.

CHAPTER 5

Let's Talk about Sex, Baby

―

Sex... As soon as we learn it exists, it pretty much takes over our bodies and minds. Let's face it. It's a bit of a mess. If you are a female, it's even a bigger mess! As soon as sex rears its ugly head in our lives, generally it's stud status for a male to be sexually active. As a female, typically, you are stuck between a rock and a hard place.

If you are one of the first to have sex, you are a slut. If you are one of the last, you are a prude. And along with that, of course, you want to be considered attractive, get attention, and have a boyfriend. It's a pickle. You also want to look sexually appealing… another pickle. If clothes are too revealing, you're a slut. Cover up too much, you're a prude. Though today I am not sure prude clothing can be found compared to when I was young! My parents never even mentioned sex to me ever. *Zero* sex talk. The only time sex was ever brought up was a quick conversation I had one night when I was fourteen after I went out with friends and came home smelling like beer.

My mom said, "Have you been drinking?"

I said, "*No!* Someone spilled beer on me!"

She said, assuming I was drunk and more likely to spill beans, "Have you had sex?"

I was horrified! The thought had never crossed my mind at that point. I had made out, sure, but sexual intercourse in my mind was still for whores. "*What?*" I screamed! "*No* and I hate you!"

That was the end of that. What's a girl to do?

As I mentioned, as far back as I can remember, which is like the age of two, I always liked boys. Having no father figure active in my life, I craved male attention. My mother also was a *tremendous* flirt, and I followed in those footsteps. I was generally pretty boy crazy, and it consumed most of my thoughts and time.

Teenage boys want one thing… sex. I wanted boys to like me, which left me feeling compelled to oblige at least in some way. And then afterward, I felt… well… yucky. I never had the confidence or self-love to stick up for myself and just say *no*.

My first sexual interaction was in sixth grade. Well, I laid there like a limp rag hating it, but I wanted him to like me.

Did he? I have no idea, but he told the whole school. Then in ninth grade, the super cute basketball player put my hand down his pants. *What is that hard, hot thing?* Horrified, I squealed and pull my hand away. That was the last of him.

At the freshman formal, that same boy from sixth grade decided we should have sex. I still don't think I'm sure if we actually did it, but I was miserable afterward. Of course after that, he went out with someone else. Then there was the boyfriend in tenth grade, who I did agree to have sex with in hopes that he would keep going out with me. He was eighteen, and it just went along with the territory. I stared at the ceiling, hating it. We did keep going out, so I guess it helped me achieve my goal? However, that kind of relationship really is for all the wrong reasons.

That was the beginning of my sexually active life. I agreed to a lot of things along the way I really didn't want to do, but because I wanted to be accepted, loved, and stay in relationships, I did them. Rather than stick up for myself I did what I felt I needed to do to keep my boyfriend. For me, sex was love. I had sex with people because I loved them, or did I love them because I had sex with them? Who knows! But it was all connected. Sex = love!

When I think back to why I chose to say yes to the man I married, it was because we had fun and had good sex. That's about all that mattered when I was twenty-one. I actually wanted to have sex more often than he did. He played professional hockey, and that came first. No sex was allowed the night before a game, which left me feeling rejected.

I never really spoke of what I liked or didn't like or wanted or didn't want. It was good, but it could have been better if we communicated. Sex somehow was a form of reassurance to make sure my partner stayed around and stayed happy. I believed it was necessary to keep a relationship healthy and keep myself in good standing.

Somewhere along the way, after I got divorced, I was finally able to just have sex without having a serious relationship. Prior to that, I only was going to have sex with someone I wanted to be in a long-term relationship with. I had ended one of my crazy relationships and hadn't had sex for like a month, which, for me, was crazy long.

My good male friend said, "Jill, you are a hot girl. Go to the bar, find a hot guy, and have sex!"

I was horrified.

"I can't have sex unless I love someone," I said.

"Try it!" he said.

Off I went to the bar with some friends. Found a hot guy. Went home with him. Had sex. Didn't fall in love. Um… I liked this. And I had a great roll for a couple years of just having fun, honoring myself, my values, and what I wanted to do. Not trying to fix anyone, or be accepted by them, and just doing what I did for myself.

Unfortunately, someone came along and ruined that. I was having a lot of fun and not allowing myself to get attached.

I was busy with work and kids and just needed sex when I needed it. It was fun having a choice and feeling more in control than I felt when "in love."

Then one of those men I was having fun with, who I was actually trying my best not to get attached to, decided we should be exclusive. I knew he was a player, but I didn't trust myself, as usual. More to come on him later.

The whole fun sex segment of my life totally changed my point of view on relationships. First, I realized that almost every single man I knew would likely have sex with me if I asked him to, whether he was in a relationship or not. Even my best friend's husband would if she approved. I realized many of my male friends really were just in it hoping to get a good shag. It's just how men are wired.

I had a customer who became a great friend, and we would talk about relationships all the time. We went to lunch the day after my son's married soccer coach hit on me out of nowhere.

I said to him, "I just realized something. Every single man I know would have sex with me if I asked him. Married or not! Relationships are just a scam!"

He said, "And you are just realizing this *now*? Marriage was invented when people lived to be fifty! Nobody can manage to be together and exclusive for fifty plus years!"

I started to realize how differently men and women view sex. Most women have a tremendous emotional connection when having sex. Why? "Oxytocin is a chemical released in both men and women after we have sex, just in very different doses" according to *The Elite Daily*.[1] "Women are programmed to become emotionally attached as a survival method."[2] This causes women to have a sense of attachment to someone they barely know. "Perhaps this could explain why we hear so many women referring to that mysterious 'connection' they felt, while simultaneously ignoring huge red flags that should make them want to run the other way."[3]

That would be my relationships in a nutshell. I always got attached, always aimed to have very long relationships, whether they were good for me or not.

The therapist I saw while I was in a relationship with a sex addict said that exact thing to me. "Jill, it's a wonderful trait that you see the good in people and try to see things from their point of view. But you don't see the big red flags you need to see to protect yourself."

Years ago, a cousin of mine was married but getting all hot and bothered about a contractor working at her office. "Just once," she said. "I need to have sex with him just once."

I said, "It's going to be like Oreos. You can't eat just one. You will get hooked."

He was in his late twenties and was engaged to be married soon. She was around forty. She had always been gorgeous, had lots and lots of sex with lots of hot guys, and being married for years that excitement goes away. She did it. And guess what she said?

"We had such a connection!"

"*You* had a connection," I said. "He had a notch on his stick for shagging a hot older chick."

Needless to say, he became distant and got married. We long for that acceptance, that connection. That makes it hard to say *no* and turn away the requests we may not really want to fulfill, but many times we do in order to be accepted.

I was out one night chatting with some ladies at the local bar. One of these ladies had quite the situation. Her husband of thirty years still feels it's her duty to give him blow jobs. And if she doesn't, he is nasty to her. She turns him away until, finally, she can't take the treatment, and she gives in. Why? The fear of rejection? Of him walking away? Of abandonment? Or just to keep the peace? Why don't we choose self-love? She would love to fix him and for him to understand this is wrong and unfair and for him to change and understand her point of view. But he won't. Why does he have to? We all get into this rut in some way, shape, or form in our relationships. I know I certainly always have.

Many women are not confident enough to set boundaries, ask for what they want, or tell men what they like and don't like during sex. Then it becomes a vicious circle of men wanting it, women not wanting it, and on it goes. But the reality is men don't know what we want unless we tell them.

It's a catch twenty-two because if we tell them, they can get all butt hurt and take it personally that we make a suggestion for something different. But we must choose the right words, including praise and just being honest. We always think that by giving men what they want sexually, they will stay with us, love us more, change, and become more of what we want them to be. Then we will live happily ever after. But the reality is, that doesn't guarantee anything.

By standing up for yourself and your desires, you will create a stronger and more respectful relationship. I am not saying the women are always the ones in this rut, but it definitely is a more common dilemma among women. Often in a relationship, when a partner finally says no and walks away, the other partner comes chasing after them. Sometimes they will change, but it would have to be because they decided to and wanted to on their own for it to be a long-term change. If not, they probably aren't the one for us. That's the hard reality for us to face.

The only path to that happy, fulfilling relationship is to stick to your values and stand up for yourself. If you have the one who really loves and respects you, he will still be there standing by your side.

CHAPTER 6

Men, Men...

Men—the poor choices and decisions I have made. But each one was here to teach me a lesson. After all, what doesn't kill ya makes ya stronger. Earlier, I had mentioned, "Fatherless daughters may struggle with trust issues, fearing abandonment or rejection."[1] This can cause the need to seek validation and acceptance, relying on others for self-worth, making them vulnerable to unhealthy relationships and codependency.

That was me from the minute I was in any type of relationship. I have learned a lot but still have a long way to go. After my last long relationship, I started on the road to relying on nobody but me for self-worth and acceptance. My horse really helped me over the hump, but I still—and probably always will—have work to do.

After learning to stick up for by boundaries and not give in to my horse, I now am able to do the same with my relationships. My friends always hated everyone I had a relationship with and now tell me that anyone I ever date again must go through a screening process.

And though they say you date people like your dad, I *never* did… or so I thought. Most partners I have had usually didn't have a job and barely made money, which is totally unlike my father. I also am all about the chemistry. They had to be hot, and I had to feel those jitters!

But let's start from the first "relationship," if you could call it that. I was twelve and in sixth grade. I already mentioned that God gifted me with the biggest boobs in the school, and with that came the cutest boy in the school, Aaron, who wanted to get at them. I couldn't believe he liked me. He came over to my house. Our parents thought it was cute. After all, we were only twelve.

We went in the basement to play Ouija board, which moved by itself, but none of my friends would ever believe that. We began asking it questions, and I could feel him trying to move it himself. He then asked it if we should make out and pushed it over to *yes*.

This was my first French kiss. How excited I was! Until he wanted to take off my clothes. I let him in hopes he would like me. I was horribly uncomfortable as his mouth moved all around my body. I wanted to cry but figured this must be what we should do. After all, my parents never ever mentioned sex to me. My dad didn't even talk.

I thought I loved him and thought we would be boyfriend and girlfriend. Instead, he told everyone what we did. His sister was a few years older than us, and he told her friends, which resulted in the news spreading like wildfire even in the high school. Of course, I had quite the reputation going into seventh grade. He broke my heart. That was the first time he broke my heart, but there were many more to come.

In ninth grade, we went to the freshman formal. He was now the school soccer star and the school heart throb with great blond soccer hair and blue eyes. We all got hotel rooms to go to after the dance, and somehow our parents were okay with this.

We were with my best friend and her boyfriend. We all made out quietly in the dark. He coerced me to have sex. I said no a couple of times but finally gave in. I loved him still… at least whatever a fifteen-year-old girl thinks love is. I figured now we would be boyfriend and girlfriend. He told everyone again, but that wasn't the end.

His parents owned a tanning salon. We would go there and make out sometimes. He moved up the road from me. Sometimes we would make out at his house. Sometimes at mine. I was never his girlfriend. I kept doing what he wanted, hoping one day I would be. I never was.

When I was a senior in high school, I thought he would ask me to prom, but he asked one of my best friends. I was heartbroken. When Aaron was going away to college in another state, he asked me to come with him and his family to drop him off. I couldn't say yes because I was dating this boyfriend who hated him. I wanted to say yes.

He invited another girl when I didn't go, who he ended up marrying later in life. When I went off to college, he would come get me and take me home to see my family. Despite all the weirdness we had been through, we remained close, almost like brother and sister in some ways.

At my wedding, his dad told me while he danced with me during the bridal dance that he thought I would be his daughter-in-law one day. I laughed, saying I did too! When I got pregnant, living in England, Aaron called me to congratulate me. When I got divorced and moved back, I found out his wife had cheated on him, and he was brokenhearted. He came over to my house I had just bought and moved into. You can guess what happened next… we had sex.

It was awkward, like it always had been. And that is when my crush finally ended. We remained close friends, and we are still very close today. His family is like a second family to me, and his sister is one of my best friends. But our relationship was actually very unhealthy for me. I suppose once I got into a serious relationship with my to-be husband and wasn't continuing to look for his acceptance, that started to change. It really wasn't until then that I was more respected by him as someone who was important in his life.

I had a few other boyfriends here and there throughout my junior high and high school years, but I was pretty much focused on him. As a result, I didn't give any of the nice boys the time of day. I dated one, Johnny, who was so very nice. Of course, I didn't like him for long. He was nice. I broke his heart when I broke up with him.

My mom invited him over to have her cheesecake, which was his favorite, and forbid me from coming home while he was there. She never talked to me at all about why I broke up with him or at all about the relationship. She just said he was such a nice boy and what a shame I didn't want to go out with him anymore.

Johnny and I still talk occasionally. He always mentions that I broke his heart. He is a superb human, and of course, one I threw away.

My next serious boyfriend, David, came along in an odd way. I was sixteen and my very best friend was dating a guy who was a senior. I had a great crush on his best friend, but he didn't seem overly interested in girls though we did a lot of kissing here and there. One night, we were at a concert at Blossom, an outdoor music venue we went to every weekend. We were stumbling around drunk on the lawn while Foreigner played "Waiting for a Girl Like You," and suddenly someone's lips were on my mouth kissing me. I heard my friend squeal my name. I opened my eyes and realized it was her boyfriend, David, kissing me!

She didn't care, though, because she really liked some other guy, so David and I ended up dating. Go figure. David was a six-foot-five total stud who looked a bit like Dolph Lundgren. He was also a bad boy and a pothead. We drank. We got high. We partied like rock stars. We made out, and he just assumed we would have sex the first time we made out. After all, he was eighteen.

I said, "Ummm, not yet!"

He acted confused and said, "We can't just stop now!"

I said, "Yes, we can."

Well, that worked once. The next time, his dad was outside mowing the lawn, and I knew I had no choice, at least not if I wanted to keep him for my boyfriend. We had sex as I stared at the ceiling, hating it. However, I learned to love it with him and also learned to hate blow jobs.

He insisted upon them occasionally, and I obliged to keep the relationship intact! Eventually, he cheated on me, became extremely jealous, punched my car ceiling… and the list goes on. But he was hot. He was my boyfriend, and I wanted it to stay that way. Sex kept him happy. I liked it, so we shagged like bunnies in the backs of our cars at a little secluded lake as often as we could.

My mom loved him and flirted with him like crazy. My friends all hated him. He was somewhat abusive though I didn't realize it. He wouldn't let me go out with my friends. One of my best friends, who I was supposed to room with in college, dropped me as a roommate because I was dating him. As a result, I had to room with strangers. I knew he was cheating on me while I was in college, so I started dating a cute hockey player, Chad, who later became my husband.

David and I didn't really keep in touch. But his mom and I were very close, and his mom was close to my mom. One time, I was home visiting from England. I went out to run an errand, and when I came home to my parents' house, my kids were gone. "Where are the boys?" I asked my mom.

"With David," she said.

"*What?*" I exclaimed, in total shock and not happy about this.

"He is in town visiting from Alabama and wanted to see them and you," she said.

Like I said, she always loved him and flirted like wildfire. He returned with my kids. They had gone to the park. He flirted with me, trying to be impressive. He had married the girl he cheated on me with in college though he has no idea I realized this. He left shortly after, and I didn't hear from him for years though I did stay in touch and see his parents frequently until they moved to Alabama with him.

About five years ago, he started following me on Facebook, liking all my pics, posting interesting comments, and all that jazz. Last year, he said he needed to speak to me. His father had passed away, and his mom was ill, so of course, I obliged. I didn't want to hurt his feelings or be mean. He announced that he had always loved me more than anyone else, though he didn't know it back then, and I was the best girlfriend he ever had.

He felt the need to apologize for being a bad boyfriend. In my mind he was one of the best, as you will agree when you learn about the others. He recently came to town and hoped to see me and my parents. Well, he saw my parents, but I was strong enough, thanks to Jack, to look out for myself. Seeing him really wouldn't have been in my best interest. I still hear from him, of course, and that's okay. He is a good person and did what he needed to do for himself by apologizing, and I do respect him for that.

Back to how I met my husband Chad. I went to Ohio State and lived in Drackett Tower. It was great because we had boys and girls in the same building. I had the boyfriend, David, at the time. At Ohio State, there were a *lot* of hot guys!

The first one who interested me was a gorgeous blond model in one of my classes named Mark. I stared at him every single day, thinking he would never like me. But one day on break, he came to talk to me. I was delightfully flustered thinking, *Oh my god, does he like me?*

We were talking away, and he said, "The freckles on your chest are sexy."

I nearly died! *Holy shit he likes me?*

I always lacked self-confidence and never thought I was good enough for the guys I really liked. Maybe this is why I was always settling for ones who didn't treat me right and was never interested as much in the nice ones. Who knows?

We hung out and did homework together. He never tried to make out, which I felt was odd and some form of rejection. I am sure he was just a nice, respectful guy, but I wasn't used to being treated with respect. Meanwhile, back at Drackett Tower, we had this big area where we all sat out in the sun.

I was in my bikini sunbathing with my roommate and her boyfriend's roommate, who was a hockey player named Roy. He had a crush on me and told the hockey team I was his girlfriend. I didn't really like him but was being friendly.

Along came a very cute, loudmouth, confident teammate of his, who apparently liked to steal the other guys' girlfriends, named Chad. He hit on me big time. He was a cocky thing who apparently was banging the whole dorm. Well, I liked him! Of course I did. He asked me out to a party.

While we were there, I turned around, and he was kissing another girl. Instead of leaving, I felt the need to win him over, get his approval, and conquer this cocky, hot guy. I went back to his dorm with him, where he announced to me that if I didn't have sex with him within two weeks, he would be having it with someone else.

What did I do the next time we went out? I had sex with him. We went out the rest of the quarter. Then summer came, and we both returned home. He went home to Canada, and I went home to David! Yep…I broke up with Chad. Upset that we split, Chad called my mom to state his case. She didn't like him when I dated him, but now she felt bad for him.

I hung out all summer with David and some old friends. The end of August came around and I went back to school to live in an apartment near the hockey arena. Chad and I had scheduled some classes together, which was uncomfortable.

He sent me and my mom sobby Christmas cards. I was pretty nasty to him. But then one day, I had a sorority sister who liked one of his teammates. I called Chad, knowing he would do whatever I wanted, and asked him to meet us with his friend.

"*No*," he said.

What the hell? I thought. *This is crazy. He said no.* Then I found out he shagged one of my sorority sisters, most likely to make me jealous. Well, it worked. That night, we saw him and his friends out at the bars, and I went back and had sex with him afterward. He drunkenly told me one day we would get married and move to Europe. I was hooked. I was determined he would be my husband, but first I needed to fix him because he was very distant, very unemotional, and very self-absorbed. He told me he didn't share his feelings with people, and if I died, he wouldn't cry at my funeral.

Well, I am going to fix that, I thought. And the mission began.

I graduated in three years because he was a year older and was going to have to leave to play hockey. We got married when I was twenty-one and moved to England—Was that fate way back then or what?—where he played professional hockey. He became super famous there, and girls would cry when they saw him and want our autographs. It was crazy!

Our relationship pretty much revolved around sex. I always wanted it more. I was like the husbands, complaining about not getting enough. He had rules about sex before games… it was not permitted. My first two relationships put me in a place where I suppose I looked at sex as a way to keep my partner happy and from straying, but I also loved it.

I'm not sure why I felt this was a way to keep a partner loyal, seeing David had cheated on me. I got pregnant five years into our married life in England, accidentally.

When we had our baby, one of his teammates said to him, "Can you believe how much this changes your life?"

He said, "Not mine. It's pretty much the same."

And that is him in a nutshell. Nothing changed his life because his life was about him. Though he behaved the same way toward me before we had children, when he neglected his children, it started to really get to me. He was never there, never spent time with them and was full of broken promises.

I had loads of attention from other hockey players, who I felt attracted to, and knew I needed to leave. I felt bad, felt sorry for him, wished I would come home and find him with someone else so I didn't have to hurt him. I knew he wasn't listening when I said I was going to leave and was going to be shocked when I actually left. And he was.

I asked him to see a counselor to try and fix things. I went on my own to figure out if I really didn't love him because he wouldn't agree to counseling. I couldn't even stomach the thought of kissing him. This was the point in my life when I learned the opposite of love is not hate. It's indifference. If you feel enough to hate, you feel! I just didn't care anymore. I told him I gave everything I had in my pot, and he never filled it up with anything from his. Mine was empty.

Why did I ever marry him? He was my boyfriend, the sex was good, and he was moving to England, so I would never see him again. And I loved him, despite the fact he was a disrespectful ass. But why wouldn't he be? After all, what you allow will continue. When people found out we were getting divorced, some would say some unpleasant things about him. I told them that none of that was why I was leaving. He was the person I chose to marry, and he was not a bad person. He just wasn't my person, and I didn't love him anymore.

Since being married to me, he has had four more kids to three different baby mamas. I never spoke poorly of him to his kids. They could assess for themselves, and they did. He moved to the US, and I was nice enough to let him live with us for a while. My older son quickly learned his selfish ways. The younger one tolerates everything, and as a result, they got along fine.

He had never paid the amount of child support he was ordered to pay nor helped or saw the kids much. Now they are grown up and have figured out their relationships with him. He has blocked me at times and called me names because he owes me thousands of dollars in back pay that he thinks should go away. I, again, was nice enough to go to court to get that right-sized. The judge told me I was nuts.

We are still friends. I do care about him and want him to be happy. We get along well now, despite all that went on. I feel like he's lonely, and I still want to try and fix him. But thanks to Jack, I have learned to set boundaries with him.

Instead of letting it pass when he gets nasty, I let him know I will not tolerate the disrespect nor be held responsible for his money and personal issues. I won't be bullied into enabling him by getting rid of what he owes me, which in the past, I may have done. We are finally at a point, I hope, where all of the disagreements are over, and we can move on and be supportive friends.

Relationships don't really come with a rule book either. But thanks to Jack, I am creating a set of rules and boundaries to protect my heart. I am paying attention to red flags and putting myself first rather than bending over backward or making dramatic changes in my life just to make someone else happy.

As you will see coming up, my choices got worse and worse as time went by. If I only had found Jack sooner, it would have saved me a *lot* of heartache, but I suppose I wouldn't have learned other necessary lessons.

Am I now standing up for myself and not allowing the disrespect? Sometimes. I am not totally fixed yet, but we are always learning. It's a process. I do know now that I cannot fix my partner. I can only fix myself.

CHAPTER 7

And More Men

Life after marriage began. At this point in my life, ever since my first boyfriend, I had never been single. I went from one long relationship to the next and then marriage. Now I found myself a single mom, needing to support my children and also needing to have a boyfriend. I mean, I always had one. Right?

Down the rat hole of many poor choices I went, all for the sake of finding the best, hottest guy. For me, it was my scale of acceptance in life. Did the guys find me hot? Did they want to have sex with me? Did they want to be my boyfriend? If it's not obvious yet, my choices in men always revolved around looks, chemistry, and sexual attraction. The trend continues…

When I moved back from England in the summer of 1997, my sister was dating a sweet, caring guy she was cheating on with several other guys. Not growing up with a father figure present had somewhat the opposite effect on her. I craved long relationships and she just craved a lot of male attention. Anyway, through her nice boyfriend, I met Jesse.

One scorching hot summer day, we went to her boyfriend's friend's lake house. Her boyfriend was joking with me about meeting his friend Jesse. He said they called him Tonto because of his huge dick. *Who cares!* I thought. I was all about suntanning and having fun in the lake.

About twenty people were having fun, drinking, and cooking out. The lake was gorgeous, and the day was perfect. There were some stand-up Jet Skis, which I had never ridden. I minded my business trying to teach myself how to ride this thing which was *not* easy.

Jesse to the rescue! He was super-hot, messy, and extremely tan having some kind of Native American heritage, not overly tall but with a sweet hot little body! He gave me a quick lesson, and I was an instant pro. We had an immediate attraction and hit it off like we had known each other forever.

When night fell, we all sat around a fire on the beach drinking and laughing. Jesse played the guitar, which made him even hotter, and we all sang. Later we all made our way to the lake house, and Jesse and I made our way into the same bed. That was the beginning of Jill and Jesse.

Jesse was the kindest, most respectful man I had ever dated at this point, which was not hard to achieve, but he actually was very nice. He loved to smoke pot and have sex. We did loads of that. He also *loved* my kids and was so very good to them. He showered them with attention, did super fun things, and was just exciting to be around. He lived a few hours from me. Therefore, we didn't see each other too often, but when we did, he was always very respectful and we had an awesome time.

After we had been dating for about six months, he started to become jealous. He couldn't deal with pictures of my ex and the kids being up on the wall. It led to him being jealous of other male friends I had as well. Of course, I tried to fix his issues, but you can't fix other people, as I now know. We tried to work through them, but we agreed to part ways amicably. I told him he taught me the way I deserved to be treated, and for that I was very thankful. Somehow, I let that fall by the wayside in my later relationships.

About a month after we broke up, this sex-crazed girl was feeling some withdrawal pains. As I mentioned earlier in the book, I had a friend advising me to just go for it without worrying about a relationship. This was the point at which I went out with friends and had sex with someone I wasn't in love with for the first time. I couldn't believe I could do this and not be in love. But I did it!

One and done and happy about it. I had an old high school friend I had started to hang out with at the time. She was unhappily married and wanted me to go out with her so she could break free from her hubby. She met a guitarist one night and totally fell for him. I was her excuse for being out, and we went to all of the band's gigs and practices.

The singer of the band and I were sort of forced to hang out so those two could be together. We got along well and had a lot of fun together, but it was a bit awkward how we were thrown together. He was a little clean-cut for me, as I was into messy-looking types. But he sang some gritty grunge, and we definitely were attracted to each other. One night we were abandoned at his apartment, lying in his bed drunk, and he asked if he could kiss me.

Whoa, nobody ever asks, I thought. Of course, I said yes, and well, of course one thing led to another, and *voila!* I had sex with someone else I was *not* in love with! Not gonna lie, I kinda wished it would have turned into something a little more, but it wasn't what the universe had planned. I was cool with it. He had been broken up with a girlfriend, they got back together, and life went on.

I was having fun being single when some friends came into town for Thanksgiving, and we went to some local bars in town. I was enjoying myself with a friend and dancing on the tables, which is what the bar is known for, when I spotted the most gorgeous man I had ever laid eyes on. He had stunning shoulder-length curly brown hair and striking bright blue eyes. I pointed him out to my friend, and we giggled away, drooling. I had to go the restroom, and when I came out, my friend told me this handsome god had approached her asking my name.

"What? I can't believe this!" I squealed in drunken delight. Just then I felt a tap on my shoulder…

"Hi, Jill… I'm Troy"… and that was the beginning of four years of one of the most tumultuous relationships my life has seen.

He hung out with us the rest of the night. My other friends left, and we had no ride home. He took us to a place up the road for breakfast at 3 a.m. Then we went back to my place. My friend went to bed, and we made out. It was weird and disconnected. He didn't like to kiss much. We messed around, and he wanted a blow job. I almost did it… *What the hell?* is what I think about that now. Not a good sign.

He was the hottest thing I had ever seen, though, and I thought I wanted to keep him around. The next morning he asked for my "digits" and left. I thought, *Well, that will be that.* I could not have been more wrong. He called me that night. He wanted to then hang out all the time. He told me he was like a lion that couldn't be caged, but he wanted to be with me all the time.

His friends told me he was crazy.

I said, "I know he is so fun!"

They said, "*No,* Jill… he is crazy for real!"

I didn't understand them and just blew it off. I did tell a friend that this seemed too good to be true. He was either a gift from God or a complete psychopath. He was a bit of a mystery, and I needed a bit of insight. I went to get my legs waxed by a lady who was apparently psychic… *bonus*!

I asked her about him and mentioned how great it would be if he was the one because he seemed amazingly wonderful.

She said, "Just be careful what you wish for… where attention goes, energy flows."

This is a saying I now live by! Soon I would find out exactly what she meant in the case of Troy.

As our relationship continued, I found out he had a pretty nontraditional upbringing. His dad actually owned that bar where I met him. He and his siblings watched porn flicks when he was eight. His dad brought home women when his mom wasn't around. His dad was a drug addict who brought home other homeless drug addicts. His dad got blow jobs in the basement of the bar and put Troy next in line. Clearly, his values and views of life were insanely skewed, and of course, I always would try to see things from his point of view and understand why he did the things he did.

The first time I met his dad, he was sitting in a big chair with his tighty-whities on and nothing else with a toy poodle on his lap, dunking bacon in his coffee cup with his fingers. He then pulled out a Cheech-and-Chong-sized joint and said, "Wanna hit?"

I was in shock, giggling, and Troy was horrified. Troy never had a sip of alcohol or did any drugs because of what he saw growing up. Troy wanted nothing more than to better his dad's health and get approval from him. His dad became ill six months into our relationship and ended up passing away. Troy was very distraught. I had thought about needing to end the relationship just prior to this but couldn't do it to him with all that was going on at this point. I hung in there, which turned into years.

Troy had the most kinky, outrageous sexual morals I had ever seen. He was doing all kinds of sex chat with girls on his computer, which I told him was unacceptable, but I let it slide due to his upbringing. We would see girls when we were out, and he would tell me outrageous stories about threesomes with them, sex, you name it. I was horrified.

He even tried to show me a porn flick of him and a past girlfriend, which I refused to watch. He thought it was funny and couldn't understand why I wouldn't watch it. In some ways, he was brutally honest, but these just weren't things you want to know or hear about.

He also told me that men undress every woman they see and think about what it would be like to have sex with them. Unfortunately, some of my good male friends have indeed confirmed this fact! I tried to empathize with his upbringing, the way he normalizes this, and of course I decided I could fix him, help him understand reality, and get over his daddy issues.

He was also *extremely* controlling. We had to go where he wanted to eat. I had to buy what he wanted me to buy and talk to who he wanted me to talk to. I had to pay for everything. He didn't like my kids to be around too much and wanted me to leave them with his parents. In hindsight, I know this relationship was extremely hard on my kids, but at the time I was drowning in it, unable to see the damage it was doing to me and them.

It was a wild ride of a relationship. My friends despised the way he treated me and didn't like his overall demeanor. He was very sex focused, very different and in their opinion, very disrespectful. Keep in mind, he followed my normal trends in men. I never choose anyone "normal." The men I dated usually didn't have a job and were extremely attractive… and not the most respectful humans! My mom, of course, adored him and flirted with him endlessly. My dad thought he was a drug dealer because he had long hair.

A few things happened that started to drive a big wedge into our relationship after dating for a few years. He started to have dinner occasionally with an old girlfriend. I told him I wasn't comfortable with it, and if they were just friends, I should be able to come along. He decided I was nuts and we should see a counselor. We ended up seeing two different counselors, and in the end, one decided Troy needed some help. He wouldn't take medication and insisted all of the problems were mine. I tried to end the relationship, but he just wouldn't accept that.

Then I met a guy while traveling for work in St Joe's, Michigan, who happened to be Muhammad Ali's chef. I sold conference calling services at the time, and Whirlpool was my client, based in Benton Harbor, Michigan. I traveled a lot back then to visit customers. My client warned me to stay in St. Joe's, as Benton Harbor is a bit rough around the edges.

St. Joe's is a gorgeous beach town on Lake Michigan. I was walking the beach after work when a handsome guy and his young son started chatting with me. He shared that he was Muhammad Ali's chef, which I thought was a fantastic pick-up line and certainly not true. His son started to talk about Will Smith during the filming of the movie, and to my shock, it was true!

We hit it off and chatted for quite a while. We exchanged numbers, and he said he if came to Cleveland, which they did from time to time, he would give me a call. It was an innocent relationship for me with no romance involved, though I am not sure the chef felt the same way.

A few months later, he came to Cleveland and called me to go meet him at a bar downtown. No sooner had I set off in shorts and a T-shirt, he called back and said to meet him at Morton's Steakhouse which is crazy fancy. I was horrified as I was not dressed accordingly, and he said it didn't matter because we were dining in a private room with Muhammad Ali and his crew. Of course I went to dinner! On a sidenote, Muhammad Ali asked me to marry him and is one of the nicest humans to grace this planet.

Troy was infuriated because he loved Muhammad Ali and was infuriated that he didn't get to meet him. He accused me of having the hots for the chef and being unfaithful. I explained we were just friends and had met in St Joe's. He refused to listen or believe me. He proceeded to remove all the men from my phone, and if they called, he would answer and tell them not to call me anymore.

Things were out of control. I also suspected he was cheating on me with a girl he worked with. I have found in hindsight that when your partner accuses you of something, many times they are doing that exact thing they accuse you of doing.

I told him we needed to stop seeing each other. He finally accepted the reality that I wanted to end the relationship about four months after I had first told him. I felt like a huge boulder had been removed from my back. I spent time with my kids, and we were very content.

I want to say I don't blame him for the way he treated me because I did allow it. And what you allow will continue. I dropped all boundaries to keep the relationship going because that's in my nature. I try to understand and put myself in the other person's shoes, but all it resulted in was me not feeling good about myself.

I have seen him a few times over the years. He has become a born-again Christian and is extreme in the way he was sexually extreme before. Here we are about twenty-five years after we broke up, and he still texts me randomly to see if I want to hang out. When I refuse, he always gets angry, tells me I have gotten lost in life, and he will pray for me. But… I don't block him. Why not? I don't want to hurt his feelings, and blocking people isn't just something I do.

After Troy, I steered clear of men and had a hiatus from them for about a year. I shot daggers at any man who looked at me, remembering they likely were picturing me naked and imagining having sex with me. I had some clear PTSD-like symptoms from this one. But my hormones soon began to flow, and back in the saddle I went…literally! I had the time of my life going out with my friends, shagging quite a few young hot men and *not* getting attached. I was a single mom raising two boys who played multiple sports and a sales manager with *zero* time for any meaningful relationship.

There was a brief exception when a friend of mine since first grade asked me if I would go on a double date with him and his wife and his little brother, Derek. I pictured Derek as a five-year-old because that was when I knew him but agreed. How bad could it be?

Well, Derek was *extremely* nice. He also was clean-cut with short hair, a tucked in shirt and a belt. *Not my style* in any way, shape, or form. Nothing about him was typical for me. When he asked me out again, I made an excuse that I didn't have a babysitter.

He said, "You can bring the kids."

Holy hell, nobody ever says this. It would be safe because I wouldn't have to kiss him with my kids there, so off we went. We all had fun; no harm done. Then he offered to help teach some foot skills to my eight-year-old son's soccer team that I was coaching at the time. Well, he got all sweaty and messy, and I reconsidered.

We began dating and even moved in together. It took him three months to kiss me. Sex was always awkward, almost as if he was hesitant or shy. He complained about a lot of things in his life but never tried to change them. Eventually his niceness and lackadaisical, negative attitude got to me.

He also was bothered with the way he felt I flirted. I admit I can come off overly friendly or flirtatious, but it's my personality. I broke up with him, which wasn't easy. I hated hurting him. My youngest son was very close with him. Whenever he asked why I went out with him, I always said it was because he was so nice. Unfortunately, nice wasn't my thing.

After that, I proceeded to go back to my free-spirited ways, living my busy life and just having fun with men on occasion. I even dated a pro basketball player a few times that I had the hots for and kept putting out the energy that I would meet him and I did… "Where attention goes, energy flows." Like I said, a quote I now live by.

I had a transformed view of relationships and felt like they were all fake. Everyone cheats. Men will shag anyone. I am not saying this is a fact, but it is certainly how I felt at the time. I learned from raising two boys on my own that men do not think in any way like women do about relationships or about the opposite sex.

They live their lives and aren't thinking about us every minute. Women tend to obsess over men twenty-four hours a day, many times thinking they are doing all kinds of inappropriate things. I was a sales manager at the time, managing thirteen younger women, and most of them were doing just that. They were all fretting about their boyfriends. I shared with them what I felt I had learned about relationships by this point.

1. Men need three things. Food, sex, and to be told they are awesome regularly. Jack isn't much different minus sex. He learns he does the right thing by release of pressure and giving of praise, and he repeats those good behaviors.
2. You never know what men are doing when you aren't with them, so stop worrying about it, or they will do those bad things you think they are doing. Where attention goes, energy flows. If they make you happy when you are with them, be happy.
3. Only get mad if it's a sin.

I was not getting attached, not getting hurt, and enjoying life. Until one of the guys in that fun space came along and ruined things. That relationship changed me forever… changed my life, rocked my world, chipped away a piece of my soul, and broke me to the core. I took what was thrown at me, ignored the red flags, let myself trust and get crushed. Before him, I kept trying to help my partners, to change them, to fix them until my pot was empty, and then I would leave. I was never broken up with and never overly broken hearted. Until him…

His name was Damon.

CHAPTER 8

Along Came a Sex Addict

―

Have you ever had a time in your life when you knew you were going down the wrong path, maybe walking with the devil a little, but instead of trusting your gut, you couldn't resist the temptation to go down that road to what you hoped could be paradise? That is the story of Damon.

As I mentioned in the previous chapter, I was at what I considered a good place in my life. I was around forty, a super successful sales manager, raising two extremely active boys on my own, traveling for work, sleeping four hours a night tops, and never stopping to look back.

I dedicated my life to working hard, playing hard, and raising my boys. I always said I was way too busy to date, and all I needed was a man in my bed at night to take care of some necessities. My past relationships soured me, and I believed no couples were actually happy, the whole experience was a phony front, and everyone cheated on each other. Men were fun for me. I had a few to choose from, and I was happy, not getting hurt, not being vulnerable and all was good. Until Damon…

Damon was one of the many men in my "funnel," as I used to call it. In sales, we have a "funnel" of opportunities, and I used to encourage the single young women who worked for me to live life, have a funnel of men, and not take everything so seriously. They even bought me a beer bong funnel for Christmas that year. I met Damon one night at a bar that I frequented with a good friend. The bar had a great patio. It was always crowded with loads of fun people and great music, especially for happy hours in the warmer months.

My friend and I started chatting with some fun guys who happened to be coaches for a local sports team. One of them gave me his card and told me I should come to a game after I told him I hated the sport he coached. He was super sexy though my friend hated him and said he had a bad vibe. The next day, he emailed me, offering tickets to the next game, and I took him up on it. That was the beginning of my life with Damon.

He traveled a lot for work, obviously, and worked all hours of the day and night. He would show up at my house sometimes at 2 a.m. and have to be back at work by 6 a.m. He never stopped. He was younger than me by fifteen years and had an adopted son and two other children. He wasn't married or with the mother, so he said.

I could tell he was a player. He would text asking where I was late night and then vanish. I asked him if he was playing roulette. That's what it felt like. He would show up hours late. I didn't care because I had my funnel, and I wasn't getting attached. But I liked him the most. Then one night while we were in the heat of hotness, he said, "You better not be doing this with anyone else!"

I laughed and said, "Why not? You are!"

He said, "*No*, I'm not!"

I laughed and said, "Okay."

That was the beginning of a million lies I chose to believe over the next five years. Our relationship was *all* about sex—sometimes uncomfortable things for me. But I really was into him, so I obliged. I always felt in the back of my mind that if we weren't having sex, he would get it from someone else. He also was uncomfortably flirtatious with my friends, who, of course, did *not* like him.

He moved from team to team as professional coaches do. At one point he moved in with his kids and their mother but said they were just friends, doing it for the kids. I believed him, both because I wanted to and because she was not at all what I felt was his type. Also, I was suspicious of a few other girls here and there, but he told a convincing story. I chose to believe him.

We had a lot of fun. I made him good food and brownies, loaned him too much money, and tried to be the best girlfriend in the world. As a coach, he was undernourished, underpaid, and didn't take care of his health, so of course,

I made up my mind to fix him, to help him, to make him happy and healthy. On one occasion, he was traveling and had no cash. Of course, I offered to loan him some. I had about two hundred dollars and figured he would need maybe fifty dollars for gas, so I took out the money and asked, "How much do you need?"

He took it all and never offered to pay it back. And I continued to offer, and he continued to take.

Looking back, I was a total fool, of course. He moved six hours away, and the mother of his kids moved with him because he claimed she wouldn't let him see the kids if she didn't move with him. My friend who was with me when I met him kept telling me he was bad news, but I didn't want to hear it.

The relationship made me feel bad about myself, as if I was always competing against other women, but I stayed in it. I had the need to succeed, not wanting to be a failure. It was very emotionally draining, and the only way I survived was yoga. It kept me grounded, patient, and calm.

I met his friends, his family, and his fellow coaches, which allowed me to trust his story, seeing I was not a secret. One weekend, after being together for about four years, he insisted upon us getting matching tattoos… our initials in an infinity sign. I went along with it, thinking he was joking, but he wasn't. We got them.

I assumed he would keep me a secret if he was actually with the mother of his children. Right? He certainly would *not* get matching tattoos. I couldn't have been more wrong. I supposed that was an effort to sweeten me up for the next thing that was about to happen, which tore me apart.

About four and a half years into the relationship, I was at a college tryout with my son, who was competing for a D1 scholarship as a football kicker. Damon was supposed to be there but had told me some odd story about why he couldn't attend. I was chatting with a coach Damon and I both knew, and he said, "I know Damon wanted to be here. Too bad it fell on the weekend of his wedding."

"Oh yeah it is too bad," I said as a pit formed in my stomach. I felt light-headed, furious, shocked… *What the fuck did he just say?*

I called Damon endlessly over the next twenty-four hours. My calls kept going instantly to voicemail, so I knew I was blocked. He finally called saying she planned it all without him knowing about it, and it was all last minute. He wasn't sure he was going to go through with it. I couldn't believe my ears.

This was all insanely absurd, and I was drowning in confusion, hope, despair. My poor son listened to me scream, cry, howl, and cuss a million obscenities on our six-hour drive back to Ohio. My heart never hurt like this. I couldn't believe I fell for these lies. I still didn't believe it was all true. All my self-confidence was gone.

The fact that I had believed him left me unable to trust myself about anything. I couldn't jump my horse anymore. I could barely ride him because my nervous lack of confidence made him spooky and unconfident himself. I was a mess.

A few weeks later, Damon showed up at my house. I now had the dog I mentioned earlier, Kuro, the crazy Malinois that wanted to eat people. He liked Damon, and I took it as a sign that he must be okay. Damon claimed he made a mistake, was going to get divorced quickly, was moving out of state to a new team, and his wife wasn't joining him. He even called to allow me to listen to him telling her he loved me and made a mistake marrying her. I wanted to believe him more than anything. I told him I would think about it.

He moved to a team down south where I went to visit him a few times. He bought me a ring and promised he was ending things with his wife. I really got to a point where I believed him about ninety percent, but something just wasn't right. We met in Florida, where he was scouting for new players as I was traveling for work.

He fell asleep, and I went to use the restroom. I heard a buzz. His pants were in there and his phone was in the pocket. Now I must say I am *never ever* the girl to look at a guy's phone. I think it's ridiculous, but right then I was compelled to pull it out and look. It wasn't locked, which is crazy. There in front of my eyes I found texts, messages, naked pictures, you name it. I found all this with at *least* twenty women within twenty seconds. I woke him up screaming like a wild lunatic. He claimed someone else was using his messaging platforms… blah, blah, blah.

He called one of the women, who was a player's mom, and had her tell me they were only friends. He made up every bad excuse in the book about all of this. We were both scheduled to fly back to the town he lived in and met there to resume the misery. He made up more lies and excuses that night.

The next day when he went off to work, I sent a Facebook message to the woman he called the night before, asking her if we could chat. She obliged. She also was not at all what I would consider his type and even older than me. She told me that she thought when we called her the night before that I was his wife. She told me he had a big crush on her, but she wasn't getting involved with someone who had a baby on the way.

"Okay thank you!" I told her as I got that same feeling I had when I talked to that coach about a year prior but a thousand times stronger. *What the fuck did she just say? Baby on the way?*

That was that. I booked a flight home immediately, letting him know his car would be at the airport and to never contact me again. As I was about to enter the airport, he drove up in a colleague's car and urged me to get in. I did. He told me a few lies about his wife being pregnant and how it all occurred, but then he settled on the best lie I have ever been told in my life. It went like this…

"You know how I fall so asleep sometimes and you can't wake me up?"

"Don't even try this one," I said.

"Well that's what happened," he said. "I was so asleep, and she just got on. I didn't know, and that's how it happened."

I got out of the car and never answered his calls as I cried my heart out every night. And about two weeks later, he showed up at my door. He cried on my pillow and told me about how he was raised in a battered woman's shelter. He told me about some forms of inappropriate behavior that went on with the children. He explained that he lies because he is good at it, it has benefited him, and it's all he has ever known. It occurred to me that he possibly had a sex addiction problem.

This is a real addiction, and suddenly I realized he fit the mold. The majority of the messages I found were from unattractive women of all ages. It made no sense. He was very attractive, and it just didn't add up. And you know what I knew I had to do? You got that right… I had to *fix him*! I found a sex addiction counselor in his town for him, and I went on my own to someone local, who I have mentioned in previous chapters.

His therapist had him do some tests that confirmed, yes, he was a sex addict indeed. For those of you who don't understand sex addiction or think it's not a real "thing," I encourage you to study it.

"The craving for sex is similar to cravings felt for alcohol or drugs by those who have addictions to these substances. It's an overwhelming compulsion or temptation that's so strong you feel that you have to have it. It's an out-of-control feeling, never feeling satisfied feeling or a constant battle to take control of something that's on autopilot. You return to the behavior—over and over again—despite the negative consequences."[1]

It's such a difficult addiction, considering sex is all around you and in your pants. You *cannot* get away from it in society. Like any other addiction, this ruins lives. I met with his therapist on my own once in an effort to understand how I could best help Damon. He said to me, "Have you heard of the book *Codependent No More*?"

"Yes!" I exclaimed. "I read it when I dated a previous controlling boyfriend." At this point I felt proud I had been doing something right!

"Read it again," he said sternly.

And so I did. I guess I hadn't been as successful as I had thought! My therapist helped me a lot as well. I was also part of a group that was comprised of all women who were married to sex addicts, and *me*, the other woman. They all asked why I remained in the relationship when I could easily leave since we were not married.

My therapist answered for me, "Because she loves him."

I surely did. Damon bailed on his therapist and told me he was talking to a good pastor friend instead. He wasn't getting help, and in the end, he lost his job due to this addiction. He called me with lies about the whole situation. That was the day I never answered his calls again. He still texts

ALONG CAME A SEX ADDICT · 101

from time to time, claiming he misses me and is divorced, blah, blah, blah.

Looking back, I do think he loved me. How could he not? I gave him everything he ever asked and allowed him pretty much to have his cake and eat it too. He would have stayed around forever. But did he respect me? *Not one ounce.* He used me. That's hard to say. That was hard to come to terms with… and that still hurts.

Up until that point, I hung in there until I didn't love someone anymore. I loved Damon with all of my heart but came to the realization that if I loved myself at all, I had to let him go… forever. I never did fix him. I never fixed any of them. I am not bashing them or saying they are bad people. Everyone does the best they can with the tools they have at the time. They did what I allowed. Who wouldn't? I chose to never date again, a status that remained in place for ten years. And now ten years later, I hopefully won't ever be in a place like that again because Jack, my horse, taught me to stand firm on my boundaries, say no, and protect myself.

I am finally starting to trust myself enough to hopefully make a good decision about a man. Thanks to Jack, I am strong, and I am getting there! In fact, I just may be ready to dip my feet in the relationship waters again. We shall see…

CHAPTER 9

Abusive Relationships

Abuse… It's a touchy topic that always seems to be up for opinion. Did I consider myself abused when I was in those past relationships? *No*, not at the time, but in many ways, I actually was.

What can be considered "abuse" after all? Abuse comes in many forms and from many types of relationships. It results in trauma that can last a lifetime and many times go unrecognized.

As a child, you aren't empowered to change things, nor do you know any different. A lot of children suffer mental abuse without anyone realizing it. It's one of those things that sometimes you don't even realize happened to you. Many times, you don't realize it while it's happening and may never realize how much it impacted your life.

In my case, I never even knew I was abused as a child until much later in life, as you read earlier. I really didn't think it must have impacted my life. Maybe that physical abuse didn't, but something along the way certainly did.

Many victims fall into relationships with narcissists. "They can be parents, partners, friends, bosses, siblings. No one is safe. This form of abuse goes way beyond physical and psychological injury. It strikes at the very soul of the victim, leaving them wondering whether they are literally going mad."[1]

"Those with narcissistic victim syndrome may automatically expect others to abuse them, making them more prone to doubt the intentions of loved ones. These challenges can affect romantic and platonic relationships. Individuals may second-guess what others say or look for signs of dishonesty."[2]

That quote explains where one of my paths went after dating quite a few narcissistic types. I began to doubt everyone. Friends, romantic partners, family… I doubted everyone's intentions. I suffered a lot of emotional and mental abuse in many of my relationships. Emotional abuse really breaks your core, affects your self-esteem, and makes you doubt yourself, which makes it harder to remove yourself from the relationship. The abusive personality is superb at making you believe they are right and *you* are wrong, which really makes you doubt your judgment. This is also known as gaslighting.

I suppose thinking back, many of my romantic relationships have been abusive. Usually not physical, though one was close. There was absolutely some mental abuse, but I didn't really realize it at the time. And to be honest, I don't think most mental abusers realize that's what they are doing either.

None of my relationships were at the level of abuse that many experience and don't know how to escape the situation. I once worked with someone who was in a physically abusive relationship. It breaks people to the core and leaves them in a state of total fear of the abuser yet somehow still loving them. They are always hoping their partner will change, believing they will change, and thinking they can fix them. Their behaviors are focused on keeping that partner happy so they don't get in trouble and don't get hurt.

The sad thing is that it doesn't matter how much they please their partner. The partner thrives on the abuse and the control, and it's going to happen again and again. The poor girl I worked with was always in fear, always walking on eggshells. Physical abusers somehow learn how to physically hurt someone and keep the bruises hidden. Nobody ever knows. The person being abused is stuck. If they stand up to them, they get hurt. If they tell someone else and the abuser finds out, they get hurt. On top of that, they risk losing this person who somehow, they still love and usually are hoping to fix.

Sadly, in this world, children are not safe from mental and physical abuse and often become victims. Child abuse really runs deep. Of course, a child doesn't even know this is wrong. It's their life, and they don't understand it's wrong. Thankfully, I cannot say my parents were abusive in any way. They did the best they could with the tools they had at the time, and they were in no way bad parents. They did everything they could to do what they believed was taking good care of us.

I was blessed to be able to interview a fabulous horse trainer, Brenda Hanson of Hanson Horses. I, and many others, view her as one of the most gifted, strongest, and most confident women we know. She works miracles with horses and understands them in an amazing way. She takes feral horses and turns them into perfectly behaved, happily domesticated citizens.

Many folks don't realize that she was abused throughout her childhood into her adulthood for seventeen years by a much older family friend who lived up the road. She was thirteen and he was sixty-one. He also molested his own daughter. He was somewhat of a grandfather figure in the neighborhood, which resulted in people assuming she rented a room at his house. She came to think of him as her boyfriend, and that was her life.

She said, "There was so much screaming and fighting and trauma and abuse" that she didn't realize everyone else's family wasn't the same.

Because of a divorce situation, her dad wasn't around as much as he would have liked to be. Her abuser told her he loved her, which made her feel special. He manipulated her so she was controlled without knowing it. Every time she tried to leave, he would put a wrench in it.

Horses were her happy place, her place of unconditional love and understanding. Lucky for her, he got old and started slipping, and she started to realize things weren't exactly right. She also had a dog that was her best friend and got her through these tough times. One day the dog starting limping, so she thought he had arthritis, but then she realized what was going on.

He was beating her dog. The dog ate something and ended up passing away. He told her to get over it, and that suddenly forced her to stand up for herself and get out of that situation. She thinks he likely fed something to the dog that killed him. Despite all of the hurt he inflicted on her, it took him hurting something she loved so much to be able to stand up for herself. She believes the dog saved her life.

I feel like a lot of abusive situations are very similar. People end up having the strength to get out when the abuser starts hurting something or someone else they love. They can't see what it is doing to them but are able to see the hurt it inflicts on others and that it is wrong.

I feel the lack of self-love that happens to someone who is abused causes this vicious circle. They love the abuser more than they love themselves, and at the same time in some ways hate themselves for not being strong enough to leave. It's also fear… fear they can't make it on their own, fear of being alone, fear of the unknown. And of course, lack of self-confidence and the inability to create the boundaries to keep themselves safe.

Abuse isn't always obvious or extreme. I feel like after being in a good number of outrageous, controlling, and unhealthy relationships, I now have a great sense for spotting them.

I met one friend while boarding my horse at a barn in the area. She always wanted to find time to hang out. Many times she came to the barn crying about her boyfriend. She wouldn't go into detail but shared that he just wasn't being "nice."

Well, funnily enough, she never could go have dinner, only lunch. And she *always* checked her phone and needed to answer his texts and phone calls immediately. One time I did get her out to dinner. She was so extremely on edge it wasn't even enjoyable. She kept checking her phone and had to be home by a certain time.

In my opinion, that is a very unhealthy and likely abusive relationship. She will never share much about what goes on, and it's tough for me because I feel helpless. It's difficult to help someone in a situation like this because I find that if you call it out, they will push you away.

I know when my friends used to call out certain things that they saw in my relationships that were unhealthy, I would go into denial, stand up for my partner, and somewhat push them away. No human ever was able to help me see the light. I had to see it myself. After years of awful relationship choices, I chose a path to be alone, and not date, because I didn't trust my judgment.

Jack was the best therapist I could have ever hoped for. Equine-assisted therapy is becoming a very popular option, which I will be discussing in a later chapter. But the reality is that getting out of an abusive relationship takes a lot of self-confidence, courage, and mostly self-love. The ability to create boundaries, stick to them with all your might, and learn to love being with yourself, the animals, and people that build you up and give you strength is what it takes. Don't blame yourself, and don't be ashamed. *None* of what happens in those situations is about you. It's about the abuser, their issues, and usually their lack of self-worth. And of course, try as you may, you *cannot* fix them. But... *yes*, you can fix yourself!

CHAPTER 10

The Fear of Being Mean

―

Dr. William Bixler, mentioned in an earlier chapter, specializes in treating sexual addiction and works with addicts, their partners, and family members. In a conversation I had with Dr. Bixler, I was explaining how none of my past romantic partners ever really go away. And I never block them.

He asked, "Why don't you tell them to stop reaching out and that you aren't interested in *any* kind of relationship with them?"

I said, "Well, it doesn't bother me that they reach out. So I don't feel the need to block anyone."

He asked, "Is that it?"

I said, "Well I don't want to hurt their feelings. I see no point in being mean."

He said, "Well, Jill, there you go. You need to have a chapter called, 'The Fear of Being Mean.'" And so, Dr. Bixler, this one is for you.

It's always been hard for me to say no, provide negative feedback, and maybe hurt someone's feelings. I'd rather say, "Yes I like that restaurant," that I really hate, "No that thing doesn't bother me," that really bothers me, and, "Of course I will help you," when really I do not have a second to pee… instead of just saying *no*.

I have always made it a point never to go out with any man I don't want to kiss. Why? Because I cannot bear the thought of someone leaning over to kiss me, and I have to say *no*. I don't want to make someone feel silly or rejected. This is probably also the reason why I wait until my relationships are completely at the last thread before I ever break up with anyone.

Leaving my husband was one of the hardest things I ever did in my life because I knew it was going to rip his world apart. I guess I generally don't want to let people down. Does anyone? We all crave acceptance. And being mean, well, it could cause someone to go away and never come back. Right?

Well, probably not if it's a worthwhile relationship. I don't like being rejected, but I find it even harder to reject someone else. I find myself coming up with a kind excuse if someone asks me to do something I don't want to do. I usually say I'm busy massaging animals, and honestly, 99 percent of the time, I am.

When friends ask for honest opinions or advice, I try my best to give it to them, but I may sugar coat things so as not to be "mean." I suppose it is human nature. But I know if someone gave me an honest opinion or advice I may not like, if I value our relationship, I sure am not ending it, and probably will have more trust in that person because they are confident enough to tell me their true opinion. And I will respect them more for it. Why do I find it so hard to do the same thing?

It's no different with horses. I had so many people tell me, "You aren't mean enough for a horse like Jack!"

Well, no, I am not "mean" enough for anything, to be honest. I spoke with one of my favorite and most admired horse trainers, Adam Black, about this subject.

He said, "It's not at all about being mean. It's about standing your ground with what you are asking them to do. It doesn't take a lot to say, 'No, no thank you, not right now. You can't come over to see me because I didn't ask.'" And then thirty seconds later you can say, 'Okay, now you can come over to see me.' And they learn that quickly."

Nothing could be truer. Animals are brutally honest, smart, and looking for that leadership. Telling them *no* and asking them to respect your space is not being mean. It's being a leader and being clear about your expectations—about what's acceptable and what's not acceptable. People really are no different.

I also found this difficult with my children. I couldn't bear to see them disappointed or upset, especially if it's a result of me being "mean." I didn't set boundaries enough for them to understand the behavior that will get good results versus negative results. I probably tried my best not to be mean and ended up not giving clear enough direction or leadership to establish the healthy, respectful relationship I desired.

Now that they are grown, they don't really ask me for advice, and I don't think they respect my opinion or see me as a leader. Not only was I weak in disciplining them, but they saw my weaknesses in my relationships with men and watched me stay with partners who didn't treat me right. I know my oldest son feels I did a poor job parenting. He doesn't really elaborate, but I am sure if I had set more boundaries and been a little more "mean," things may have been different. One never knows…

When I was a sales manager, it was always difficult for me if someone was underperforming to the point I had to let them go. I know how upsetting and life-changing losing your job can be, but it also isn't doing anyone a favor to keep them in a job where they cannot be successful. And, of course, I didn't want them to leave with bad feelings about me and never wanted to be considered "mean."

I have agreed to see old boyfriends after years because I don't want to be "mean" and don't want to say no. And it's gotten me into some predicaments. I think especially when we are talking about situations with members of the opposite sex, it's easy for women to give the wrong vibe just by being "nice."

I agree to breakfast or lunch, and the next thing you know, they think I want to be back in bed with them. It's like getting stuck between a rock and a hard place. This happens frequently with Troy. He reaches out and messages me. I try not to reply. He keeps messaging, and then finally I think, *Well, I don't want to be mean, so I will just reply. What if he is depressed, or who knows what is going on in his life?*

It never fails that once I reply, he asks to get together, which I am *not* going to do. I have done that before, and it didn't end well. So I tell him I am busy, and he gets furious saying I should make time for things that are important. The reality is that I don't even see some very close friends who are very important because I really do *not* have much free time.

For some reason, I explain myself to him. Why do I feel the need to do that? But it doesn't matter what I say. I end up being the bad guy because I didn't want to be mean!

The most recent time this occurred, I responded differently, thanks to my lessons from Jack over this last year. I was much more direct. And he got mad… but then he came back a week later trying to be nice. Point proven. He didn't go away but returned trying to make amends and maybe having more respect for me because I stood my ground and was direct… *not mean.*

It was always like that with Jack. I would think, *I don't want to be mean. I don't want to upset or hurt him.*

What I learned from another one of my favorite horse trainers, Carson James, is that horses don't consider it to be mean. It's what they crave. They crave direction. They crave boundaries. They crave leadership. And that's *exactly* what I found with Jack.

When I was wishy-washy with my asks, unsure if I was being too mean and doubting myself, he would push me around, kick out a leg, rear… You name it, he tried it! But when I said,

"No, we won't do that right now," and meant it, he respected me for the boundaries.

He felt more confident because I was confident, and as a result he felt safe to follow me. And I didn't have to be harsh, or rough, or mean. I just had to stand my ground and be confident.

Interacting with people is actually no different. Being confident and standing up for yourself is not being mean. It's respecting yourself and your boundaries and letting people know them. The outcome isn't that they think you're mean. They think you are strong, confident, and worth respect.

CHAPTER 11

Raising Children

"We never know the love of a parent, until we become one ourselves."

—HENRY WARD BEECHER

My mother always told me when I was growing up, that one day I would have a child exactly like me, and I would see what it's like being a parent. And I guess that's exactly how life goes. You dedicate your life to making sure your kids have everything they need and want, trying to keep them happy, and loving them unconditionally. And in return you hear…

"I don't like you! I never liked you!"

"You ruined my life!"

"You're stupid!"

Should I go on? You know deep down, they love you. They don't have to like you. But you often wonder where you went wrong.

Being a parent is inexplicable really. I remember when I was pregnant with my first child, my uncle said to me, "Honey, you think you love your husband. That love will be nothing compared to the love you will have for this baby!"

I told him that was pretty much hogwash. That I loved my husband more than the universe, and I would love my baby equally. I couldn't have been more wrong. The instant my baby was born, I felt a love like never before. This small gorgeous, fragile little being. I made him. I had to protect him from this world forever. I remember when we left the hospital feeling a slight panic that he was now going into the real world. He could get germs, get sick, get hurt, which was all unimaginable!

We barely knew what we were doing in our own lives, and now we were in charge of raising another human. All you want for your child is for life to be perfect, painless, and full of joy. If only we could make that happen. I vowed to *not* be like my parents, to not to be so judgmental and critical, and to be more involved in what's important in my kids' lives… to lift them up and give them confidence.

My first child, Cory, was born two weeks late. He clearly knew this world was a tough one. He was wide awake and a perfectly beautiful china doll. He never wanted to sleep, nor did he want anyone to touch him other than me. I was bound and determined to do everything right.

My husband was never around so I pretty much raised him on my own. He was my world, and I was his. My second baby, Josh, was born a day early and rushed into the world easily.

These boys were totally opposite from day one. Cory was inquisitive, watchful and somewhat untrusting of the world from the start. Josh was carefree and lighthearted.

Cory was two and a half when Josh came along, and he wasn't overly happy to have to share his world with this new baby. He poked him in the eyes when I wasn't looking and did his best to keep my attention on him. Josh was much more laid back than Cory was and actually slept! They were my entire world as a young mom, living in a foreign country and moving every year to a different hockey team in a different location.

I always wanted to be sure they were getting the best of everything. They were breastfed as long as possible. I made them homemade baby food. We did playgroups, baby gymnastics, playdates. You name it, we did it. When they were five and two and a half, I left my husband and became a single mom, and they remained the most important things in my world.

I moved back to the US and in with my parents for almost a year. But at the same time, I needed to focus on my job to be able to provide for them, I was also focused on men! Unfortunately, I hadn't yet realized I didn't need them. Looking back, I wish I had just focused on my children, but you don't know what you don't know.

I ran a million miles an hour all day every day, slept for maybe four hours a night, and time just flew by. I took them to all their practices, games, and activities. I made their breakfasts, lunches, cooked dinner every night. I helped them with their homework, and heck, sometimes I even did it for them. I wanted them to be happy, healthy, strong, popular, get good grades, and the list goes on. It was very difficult. I thought my focus was all in the right places, but I suppose my sons would disagree just like I do about my parents.

Their dad lived in England and didn't play a part in their lives. He would call once a week and tell them about his hockey game. The day after Christmas every year, I would take them to England and leave them with him for a week. It was the only way they would ever see him.

He didn't help financially, so I was focused on being very successful at my job. I didn't want my kids to have to go without, and they never did. I had a few different relationships, and I don't think any of them went over well with my oldest son. He was very protective and likely knew better than I did at the time that those men were mostly bad news.

He was an intuitive child though I didn't realize it back then. I don't really think he liked me seeing anyone. Looking back, maybe I shouldn't have exposed them to my partners, but then how do you build a serious relationship with someone if you don't involve them in your home life? If you don't see how they fit in with your family? It's all such a complicated road to travel.

I gave my boys everything they ever wanted when they were growing up. I didn't set good boundaries or rules and was a terrible disciplinarian. One time while we were out, the boys really misbehaved. I told them when they got home, they would have time outs and things taken away. Well, of course, we got home and I forgot.

Josh came up to me about thirty minutes after we got home and said, "Mom, aren't we supposed to be in trouble?"

That is Josh in a nutshell. Josh is like an old, all-knowing soul. He's a sensitive artistic type who is not afraid to share his feelings and speak his mind. He was always very sensitive to everyone's feelings. Despite the fact his brother picked on him relentlessly, one day at McDonald's when Cory asked Josh for his last chicken nugget, Josh sadly looked at his nugget and handed it over to Cory. That's Josh.

Cory, on the other hand, keeps things in. He was extremely difficult to punish because he just didn't care or show he did. I could take all of his favorite things away, and he didn't care. He also was super sensitive but would never show it.

Cory also dedicated a lot of his time to teasing and harassing his brother. Josh wasn't a fighter, thank god, so they had almost no fights. Josh was bigger than Cory, even though he was younger. Cory would hurt his feelings over and over again. Now, this can drive a parent to the brink of insanity, and that it did to me!

Around the age of thirteen, Cory had a brief time when he thought it was funny to spit on Josh from the hallway above our family room. Josh would whine, resulting in Cory persisting. I was at my wits' end, and I told Cory next time he spat on Josh, I was spitting on him. I was cooking dinner and heard *splat…*

I turned into Wonder Woman. Cory spat from upstairs about twenty feet from his bedroom door. I turned and flew from the kitchen, up the stairs and got to his bedroom door right before it shut. He ran to lie on his bed. I jumped on to him with my knees on his shoulders and spat right on his face.

He cried, "Mooooooommmm, *gross!*"

I left his room, out of breath, realizing I was completely insane. I suppose it's not hard to believe he never spat on Josh again.

Josh was twelve when I broke up with Derek, and that breakup hit him hard. Derek was the nice guy I dated and moved in with… the one I chose to date because he said I could bring my kids when I made up the excuse that I didn't have a babysitter. Josh played soccer for him while we dated, and they had quite a bond.

As I mentioned, Josh is an artist and an old soul who showed his sensitivity from a young age. Cory, on the other hand, would keep it in and let it turn to anger. Cory didn't care for Derek or any of the men I dated, for that matter. Being intuitive, he likely could see things I just wasn't wanting to admit.

Cory was about fourteen at this time, and he became painfully sad and upset that his dad wasn't here in the US or around like other kids' dads were. He never really understood why his dad and I didn't stay married, and I think he always blamed me and probably still does. Their dad moved back to the US around this time, and my sons could make their own assessments of him.

Cory found it hard to accept and understand his father. We all went to a counselor to try and work through issues, and he said they were well-adjusted, normal kids doing well working through what life has thrown at them. The counselor told their dad that he couldn't just walk back into their lives, order them around, and be their dad after all those years. He had to *earn* it. After that, their dad refused to ever go back to counseling.

Regardless, I was the punching bag in my sons' world… and I still am. They never ever tell their dad what they think of him. They never ask him for help or money. I am their rock, and sometimes I think they hate me for it. I went to a counselor on my own to try and understand how to best interact with Cory. I was worried about him. He seemed depressed and, of course, wouldn't talk to me about anything.

It hurt me to my core to see him this way. The counselor told me to set aside certain times to think about him instead of thinking about him too much. I thought that idea was absurd! He also told me to not offer him any help unless he asked for it since he got mad when I offered and never did what I suggested anyway.

I try to follow that advice to this day, but Cory is a tough one. I never set boundaries when he was younger. I gave too much, tried to fix too much, and ended up in a place where I am disrespected just like I was in my personal relationships.

But he is an adult now. I can't fix him… I can only fix myself.

Josh isn't as tough to understand. He is more up front about his feelings. He has a quick temper, but we get along. He is more easy-going just like when he was a baby. But does he respect me? Not totally. He doesn't really take time to listen to what I say and sometimes just flies off the handle. Regardless, I love them both equally and more than anything in this universe, more than anything I have ever loved.

I am extremely proud of my boys. They grew up to be successful, strong, determined men. I guess I did something right. But our relationships, well, I wish I could change them in a lot of ways. I wish they would talk to me about their lives, share their feelings, ask my advice and have real conversations. My parents didn't with me, and I suppose I didn't with them. I swore I wouldn't be like my parents, and I don't think I was, but I must have done something the same.

My boys and I can't really have serious conversations. They get mad and yell. They say I ask too many questions or they don't want to hear what I have to say. I don't know why or what I did to make things this way, and I probably never will. I just hope as they grow older, it will change.

I couldn't do this parenting thing without that crazy, unconditional love that comes over you when you see your baby for the first time. Parenting is truly the hardest thing in life. You never know if you are doing the right thing, and it *never* ends. Even today as they are adults, parenting—worrying about them and if you did it right, if you are still doing it right—never ends.

I have no regrets and would definitely do it all over again because it is also one of the most rewarding things in life. But I always think, in this rat race of life while raising kids on my own, working a fast-paced sales job, and juggling personal relationships, did I do it right? Well, looking back, I would say no. I would do so many things differently.

Raising two boys as a single mom did teach me a *lot* about men and how they view the world very differently than women. If I had Jack before having kids, I am sure I would have parented *much* differently. I would have had many more boundaries and would have found it much easier to discipline. I know that would have helped me gain respect. But you can't turn back time. I tried to do it right. I did the best I could with the tools I had at the time.

I have told my kids I did my best. I loved them with all my heart, and whatever they feel I didn't do right, I am sorry. After all, parenting doesn't come with a rule book. And… parenting never ends.

CHAPTER 12

Friends or Frenemies?

I'm not sure about you, but I know I have certain friends who I think, *If I never called or texted them would I ever hear from them again?*

What exactly is a friend? Well… according to the Collins Dictionary, it is this…

1. *a person whom one knows well and is fond of; intimate associate; close acquaintance*
2. *a person on the same side in a struggle; one who is not an enemy or foe; ally*
3. *a supporter or sympathizer*
4. *something thought of as like a friend in being helpful, reliable, etc.*

It's interesting to take a close look at this—at least it is for me. Are my friends on the same side as me during a struggle? Are they backstabbing me and pretending to be on my side? Are my friends supportive? Sympathetic? Helpful? Reliable?

Thankfully, I have some friends who are those things, a few of them, a very *few* true friends. I used to think I had a lot of friends. I came to realize that many of them were only around for the good times, and when the tough times came, they were nowhere to be found. The older you get, the more you learn and understand not only about these "friends" but about yourself.

If we go way back to my school days, I guess you could say I was in the "popular" crowd and probably a bit of a mean girl. Not just anyone could be our friends. Only the cool, pretty people could be part of the crowd. We had a specific group we called "The Great Eight."

We had our own parties, hung out together, and excluded just about everyone else. I would occasionally try to bring others, which made me less than a favorite in that group. A couple of my best friends were not a part of that group, and they were the people I hung out with the most later in high school and college.

Only one person from that group is really a true, close friend today, and she has been my friend since first grade.

Another girl, who I thought was actually my best friend since first grade, seemed to lead the group. She hated worms, birds, and all sorts of things. Some of the other girls would fawn over her issues. The odd thing about that friend is that she was in my wedding and didn't even invite me to hers. See… friends? Or frenemies? Although I didn't agree with all that went on back then, I still felt the need to be accepted and be part of that group.

I still keep in touch with just about all of them in some way… mostly small ways such as Facebook. Back then I felt the biggest part of wanting to be friends with someone was about acceptance, being part of the in crowd, part of the cool people. We didn't really choose back then to be friends with someone because of the actual person they were but more because of how they looked, the sports they played, or who their boyfriend was.

I have a couple dear friends today who were my friends way back to kindergarten. We don't speak often, but we are there for each other when it's needed, and that will never change. Many of those people who were my "friends" way back then are still acquaintances today. But are they real friends?

Similarly to my relationships with men, I have had many "friends" who really weren't contributing anything to our relationship. I would do my best to try and fix them, as I have always fallen into the counseling role in my friendships. Sometimes it would be marriage counseling, sometimes raising children counseling, and sometimes how to deal with other friends counseling.

I wanted them to love me but also wanted them to be happy. I always have had a hard time saying *no* and frequently would over extend myself when the friends came calling for help, a night out, you name it. But I can only count on one hand the ones who would do the same for me. It took me all these years to realize that.

It takes a lot for me to *end* a friendship. I always keep it going in some way, shape, or form. I am not sure why. I am not really good at "ending" much of anything. I have had people I considered *very* good close friends—friends I spoke to every day, saw every week—suddenly just vanish or break up with me. One just, poof, stopped talking to me. To this day, I don't know why.

I called, texted, tried to find out what happened. Still to this day I do not know and have not heard from her. I heard it was because of something Troy told her I had said, but I would have thought she would have confronted me herself. Is that a boundary of hers, or is that being a coward? I had another friend who informed me she was breaking up with me. She told me her counselor said I wanted to party too much, which didn't work out with her goal of wanting to find a husband. She invited me to every party we had ever gone to and wanted to hang out every weekend. I would have to carry her drunk self home from the bars. Was that a boundary of hers or blaming someone else for where her life was going?

I have to say I enjoy friendships with the opposite sex most of the time over friendships with women. They are more lighthearted, fun, and much less drama-filled, less judgmental. Maybe the women remind me too much of the drama I experienced with my mother. Who knows? Unfortunately, many of those men I thought were friends really had another motive. As a result, a lot of those friendships went sideways.

I had a wonderful friend who was really more like a girlfriend. We went on trips, slept in the same bed, and did everything together. People started to comment that he was in love with me. I approached the subject with him in a lighthearted way and found out they were right.

He was bitter that I didn't feel the same way. I had another close friend who was Josh's soccer coach. Suddenly he started to make sexual advances. Many men still remain my good friends today and are some of the very best friends I have.

I ended one friendship after realizing it just wasn't good for me and my life. Then, looking back, I had to wonder, were they actually real friends? I truly loved them and thought they were. I wanted them to love me because they were cool and fun! They were a couple I met through one of my best friends. I met them when I moved back to Ohio. She moved out of state and I remained good friends with them. We hung out often.

They had frequent dinner parties, as one was an awesome cook. I traveled with them on a company trip to keep the nonworking partner company during work events. They came to my kids' graduation parties and were what I considered dear friends. We didn't really have a lot in common because they were millionaires and into buying nice things, going to extravagant places… all that jazz.

I, on the other hand, wear the same shoes and clothes for twenty years if I like them and would never consider spending thousands of dollars on a watch in my wildest dreams. In fact, I find it wasteful. Most of their friends were like them.

One of them would say, "I am going to come redo your closet and throw out most of your clothes."

"I like my clothes. I am not froofy like you guys!" I would say.

Or he would say, "Oh *my god* those shoes are awful!"

"They are my favorite!" I would say.

I thought he was teasing but never was quite sure. When I decided to move, one of their moms was going to move into an apartment, leaving her house up for sale. It was perfect for me and decorated beautifully, considering one of them was an interior designer. They had set a price, and the inspection found a few things that needed done, one being replacement of a boiler that was fifty years old.

I asked to negotiate the price a small amount. They wouldn't budge and I didn't push it since they were my friends. Well, two months after I moved in, the boiler shit the bed. It was going to cost ten grand to replace it. If I were them, I would certainly have offered to pay half of that expense, considering it was an item of contention in negotiation. They didn't, and of course, I didn't push the point, being my old pushover self. I was a bit hurt, but we remained friends.

Then one day we went to dinner at their house with my son, who had just decided to end his college football kicking career due to an onslaught of injuries—a very mature but extremely difficult decision considering that was his dream. At dinner, one of them kept pushing him about what he was going to do next and sharing that he didn't have the luxury of having an easy college life with a scholarship.

Anyone who knows the life of a college football player will know it's anything but *easy*. It's incredibly difficult. They own you. My son is pretty meek, but he spoke up and explained what it's actually like. My friend screamed at him and stormed off, saying my son was dead to him because he was disrespectful, which he was not and even his partner agreed.

I am not sure if there was a sensitive point around this, as this was very out of character for him. He was very emotional, sometimes a bit dramatic, but not to this extreme. Although I do tolerate people disrespecting me, I do not at all accept this type of behavior toward my children. I walked away from that friendship. We still see each other out and about or on social media. I miss them a lot, but that was a boundary I had to set at the time. It was super difficult for me to do.

The sad thing in the world of friends is that many people don't really like to see others succeed. I don't know why that is, but I believe it's a fact. Now I can promise you, if I have friends who start a business or set goals and are looking to achieve something, I am supporting them one hundred percent. I would support their business whether I needed to for myself or not. Sadly, I have found not many folks are that way. Does that mean they don't care and don't really want you to succeed, or does that mean they are setting boundaries? I'm not quite sure I have figured that out yet.

Since writing my introduction, my mom recently passed away. It was a bit eye-opening for me to witness the support from friends. I never ask for help or support, and I get along fine without it. However, at times like this, when you hear nothing from people, it hits a little hard. Just a kind word, even via text, goes a long way. I have my true-blue friends who, of course, were there for me in every way possible.

A couple of them called saying, "I am flying in! I will be there!"

"No, you don't have to. I am fine," I said.

I could have used their support, but I never like people to go out of their way to do stuff for me, and maybe that could even be a reason why they don't. Who knows?

Some friends I may not see or talk to for long periods of time, but they are always there for me when I need them. Then, I have friends I see more often and talk to more often who just aren't there at all. In fact, one friend I have had since grade school never said a peep for over a week—no card, no nothing—but proceeded to tell me all about the troubles with his father who was sick and had to move into a facility. Did I support him? *Yes.* Did I say anything about the lack of support I got from him? *Nope.* I didn't feel the need to, but it was eye-opening. How do I interpret that? I am not quite sure.

I used to hang out with this same friend weekly for a couple of years. Then he started dating someone who didn't like the fact we hung out. He stopped talking to me for five years. When he came back around, I didn't pressure him about the past and just enjoyed his company. He still was dating her and apparently was not telling her we were hanging out. She found out, and he said he didn't care and that we were going to remain friends regardless. Well, that didn't happen. In fact, he ghosted me for almost a year. Now in the past, I would have let that be and never directly shared how I felt about it.

I usually go out of my way to support folks, so, yeah, I have a hard time sticking up for myself and haven't quite figured it out. What I have figured out, thanks to Jack, is how to set boundaries with my friends. After being ghosted for almost a year, I dropped off a bottle of his favorite bourbon for his birthday along with a letter, explaining how his actions hurt me, and that it's disrespectful to treat a friend this way.

I said he should do what's best for him, but unless he wants to treat me with respect, I was bowing out. In the past I would have been petrified that he may never speak to me again and would never have done that. Well, guess what happened? It took him a while, but he reached out saying my letter made him realize he had been a poor friend, and he was sorry. Magic, just like when I created boundaries with Jack!

Jack taught me to create those boundaries, allowing me to be able to say *no* to outings I am invited to and things friends ask me to do that are tough for my schedule. I'm also able to create boundaries to be sure and set aside time for myself and my animals. I have been let down in many ways. I have had best friends who didn't ask me to be in their bridal party, best friends who didn't invite me to events, and best friends who don't support my business. I make it a point to *never* hold grudges, but I also never forget. You really can't forget and look out for yourself at the same time. I try to be the very best friend I can be and love my friends to the fullest… my real friends.

As for family, it's funny how people say, "family over everything." In some ways I envy those people. I could not answer yes to those questions I started this chapter with for *anyone* in my family except maybe my parents. My family never even reaches out to see how I am doing. Since my mother passed away, I haven't heard from any of them.

During the last ten years of her Alzheimer's, I rarely heard from any of them. They know nothing of my personal life or any success or troubles I have. My sister has only ever reached out when she has needed something. My father was extremely ill twice during my mom's last five years of Alzheimer's. I had to care for them both over the period of at least a month while working a full-time job. My sister did not have a job and didn't help at all unless it was convenient for her. Family... you don't pick 'em. I have a few good friends I could never thank enough for always being there, no matter what, and I consider them family.

Everyone is busy. Everyone has stuff to do. Everyone makes excuses. I have tried to no longer make excuses. Instead, I try to set boundaries and honestly explain why I am saying *no* or what I need in the relationship, just like I did with Jack. The bottom line is that all friendships are different. I make it a point to give without expectations of getting anything in return.

I give because I want to, and it makes my heart feel good. At the same time, boundaries are necessary to prevent some people from sucking all of your energy dry and hurting your heart. And when you set those boundaries, you get back much more respect from your friends, your family, your romantic interests... and your horse.

CHAPTER 13

Workplace Boundaries

Similarly to earning respect in personal relationships, there is also the matter of gaining respect in the workplace, with both clients and colleagues. I have been in sales all my life. Even before I was in the workforce, I "sold" my friends on doing what I thought was best for the situation.

That may have been staying up all night, eating an abundance of my grandma's Italian cooking or calling a certain boy on the phone. Some may have called me "bossy." I am sure a few of my longtime friends are giggling and remember exactly what I mean when they read this.

I entered the actual workplace my last year in high school. I was a fragrance model at a local department store, convincing folks they needed a squirt of the fragrance I was touting. I wanted to be like the big-time cosmetic girls behind the counter. That sentence I suppose makes a statement about most of my working career.

I always wanted to be like someone else… someone I thought was better than me. I probably was only into the cosmetic stuff because my mother was extremely obsessed with always being perfectly made up. As soon as I broke out of the "parent" mold, I started to hate all of that froof and barely wear makeup now. I was always trying to be someone I really wasn't in order to fit in, succeed, get promoted… you name it. I never thought I was the best, which I thought I needed to be. Why was that?

Well, let's remember my mother…

"Why did you get a B?"

"You can't be a model. Your boobs are too big."

"Why didn't you get the longest solo?" in the school choir concert.

I supposed this left me always feeling the need to be the best.

When I moved to England, they found me overqualified for most jobs with my college degree because going to "university" wasn't the norm. I ended up selling advertising for a local newspaper. I spent my days whizzing around country roads in Northeast England on the wrong side of the car, on the wrong side of the stick shift, and on the wrong side of the road making loads of fun friends and drinking loads of cuppas.

I love getting to know my customers and what makes them tick. Some of my best friends were people I met selling advertising back then. But I wanted to be like Bev. She was such a pretty girlfriend of one of my husband's work pals, and she was an area manager for Estée Lauder.

I have to say, I am a great salesperson and also great at selling myself to get what I want. I got a job as a counter manager in Sunderland, a small rough town in the northeast of England. I could barely understand the thick local dialect, and I was very under made up compared to the other girls. I tried to be like them and wore lots more makeup. I never really fit in though I tried my best. I did have a lot of fun trying!

When I moved back to the US, I got a job selling copiers because now I was apparently underqualified, having never worked in the US. That was one of the most grueling, difficult sales jobs *ever*. My boss was an enormous man named Herb. His sales training involved one thing. His sales strategy consisted of this… when people said they didn't want to buy a copier, you had to look them in the eye and say, "Why?"

His voice was low, and big and scary. I, on the other hand, sounded like a bunny giggling. It just didn't work for me and neither did that job. The best part of the job was a sales colleague of mine, my mentor and partner in crime. We would drive around singing, laughing, and eating burgers at a local joint called Swenson's while I made him listen to me sing Toni Braxton songs! But the pay was horrible, and I wasn't going to survive on what I made.

By a stroke of luck, I got a job selling conference calling services, which was the beginning of my real sales career. This company was a wild ride. We worked hard and partied harder. It was a race to be the VP's pet, get the top, and be recognized! It was a pretty unethical but fabulously fun culture, and for the most part everyone was wild and crazy, so I fit in well there.

I let things happen that shouldn't have, that maybe I wasn't comfortable with, in order to be part of the in group and get to the top. I felt a lot of peer pressure to drink a lot, party a lot, and do what I needed to do to get to the top. We were like a huge family, and we had an enormous blast. And then some corruption began.

I was forced to cut people on my team. One of my direct reports, who I was closest with, was targeted as someone who needed to be let go. It was awkward and uncomfortable and unfair. But I needed to keep my job, and instead of standing up to this, I went along with it. In return, she retaliated, and we both ended up losing our jobs. I was hurt and devastated. This "family" didn't stand behind me. After nearly fifteen years, that was that. I felt very betrayed and also in some ways blamed myself for not being enough in the "in crowd" and not sticking up for my beliefs.

But why would I have wanted to be in with a crowd that did these things? Well, I dearly loved the VP of sales and thought he was one of my best friends. But then everything came crushing down. People tried to convince me to sue them. I talked to an attorney and started down the path, but I didn't have the confidence to stay in the game… to stick up for myself… to stick up for my boundaries.

Most of all, I still loved that family. That VP of sales is still one of my dearest friends today, despite everything that went on. I love him like a brother. I also made peace with the friend who retaliated, and she is one of my very dearest friends today. Money makes people do things their heart doesn't want to do, and I saw the best side of them and loved them unconditionally. I still do.

After that I worked for three of the largest tech companies in the world over a period of about twelve years. I learned I am just not like most people in the world of professional sales. I am not "groomed" enough, "professional" enough. I am me. I laugh, I build relationships, I get to know people, and I am not the most reserved person. I hug, I laugh, and I love.

One of my very, very favorite bosses, who I call "G," once said to me, "Jill, people won't buy from you because they like you!"

I said, "Oh, G, they may not have the power to buy from you because they like you, but they sure do have the power to kick you down the road if they don't like you!"

Building relationships is my number one strength, and it has served me well with my customers. Oddly enough, it wasn't always as easy to do with my coworkers at these big tech companies. Many were arrogant, stuffy, and all business, which is just not my style. But I tried my best to fit in, to change, to be like the people I viewed as the best. I really would have been more successful just honoring myself, but I didn't have the confidence to do that.

One boss said to me, "Jill, what do you think is the first thing people think of you when they meet you?"

I said, "They probably think I am fun, bubbly, and not very smart."

"Well, maybe you should concentrate on them thinking you are smart!" she replied.

I was horrified, but I never told her that. I never shared how unethical I felt this statement was to her or anyone else at the company. I didn't stick up for myself. Instead, I tried to be more like them. I had another boss patronize and talk down to me regularly on internal calls to such an extreme that people used to comment about it to me privately. Instead of me calling him out on this, I tolerated it in hopes of being better liked by him. That just earned me more disrespect.

Despite that, I was always very successful, earned loads of trust, and made great friends with my customers, but it's no wonder I never loved my jobs because I was not like the rest of my colleagues. I was always trying to be something I was not in hopes of being more successful, more well-liked, more promotable.

However, the people who stand up for themselves, set boundaries, and show people they know their worth are the ones who get noticed and get the promotions. Period. Jack taught me that I need to stand up for myself, set those boundaries, and in return I will get the respect I deserve. With Jack, the little things made the big differences.

For example, when we are doing ground work, I ask him to walk but he keeps right on trotting.

Okay Jack, you don't want to listen, well then you can canter. A canter is a faster gate and harder work for him, hence next time he should choose to listen, and his life will be easier.

Or I say, *Whoa, you wait there, Jack* and he decides he will take a step toward me.

Okay, Jack, now you can back up five steps and wait longer because I didn't say to move. This again is harder work, so next time he should choose to just whoa.

The key is, when the horse does what you ask, *stop* asking. Be clear and concise in order for him to realize he has the correct answer. The release is the reward, which is key. People are no different.

After my lessons from Jack, I started to stand up for myself to my next boss. I told him things that didn't benefit me, wasted my time, and weren't productive in our daily workings. And guess what? He changed things and respected me more than any boss has in my thirty-plus-year sales career. Except for maybe G, and we are still good friends today.

I recently was part of a headcount reduction and lucky enough to get a package that allowed me to find a job that suited me. I promised myself I would only accept a job where they valued and respected me for who I am. The interviewing process was excruciatingly painful, as I was not going to answer these robot questions in a robot fashion. I put myself in charge, dismissing opportunities where I didn't feel I would get along with the person I would work for. Then along came a refreshing change. A tiny company approached me, headquartered in Israel. The man who would be my boss was Israeli and very direct. He first asked me about my animal massage business. He was the *only* person to ever even mention this. I was impressed.

We talked for quite some time and he said, "I have a direct question for you."

I said, "Okay."

He said, "I can't imagine you meeting with a CEO."

It wasn't really a question, but I was amused and impressed with his honesty. I am sure most other folks thought the same thing but wouldn't say it. I told him some of my best friends are CEOs I have worked with in past. I also told him some technology managers are much more straitlaced than CEOs, if he was referring to my laidback, carefree demeanor.

I let him know that since I would be working for him, he needed to know the real me, and that was who he was going to see in the interview process. And that I can adjust my style to match the folks I am selling to. Then I shared the story about the boss telling me I need to appear smart as a first impression. He was horrified. He asked me if I would be willing to move to the next step, a simulation where I would need to role play as if I was presenting to a CEO.

I said, "Sure!" thinking this should be a fun exercise.

He was joined on that call by his sales advisor. I did my role play, being a bit more professional, but still being me. I asked his advisor how he felt about the CEO comment.

He said, "I don't give feedback on these calls, but I think you are charming. I want to be your friend, and I think you could open doors that a lot of people can't!"

I was beside myself with delight. My potential boss said he was still wrapping his head around it and would let me know. I got a call a couple of weeks later from him, offering me the job.

I said, "So, you can now see me meeting with a CEO?"

He said, "I am not sure, but there aren't any other salespeople like you. You are exactly what we need, and we needed you five months ago!"

Yesssss! I was elated and proud! I stood my ground, kept my boundaries, and got a job that is my favorite sales job to date with wonderful, caring amazing people!

Workplaces these days are full of corruption, cutthroat, get ahead of the other guy mentalities. It's sad. Again, thanks to Jack, I had the confidence to value myself and stick to my boundaries rather than morph into something that I really am not just to please someone else.

As author Leo Buscaglia said in his book *Living, Loving and Learning*, "The easiest thing to be in the world is you. The most difficult thing to be is what other people want you to be. Don't let them put you in that position."[1] Thanks to lessons from Jack, I never will again.

CHAPTER 14

Confidence and Boundaries

I had the pleasure of interviewing Rachel Whitehawk, the founder and director of Whitehawk Ranch, an institute for cognitive resilience founded to provide women and teen girls the opportunity to achieve optimal health and happiness through working with horses. When I spoke with her, two quotes really stuck out for me.

"Boundaries equal freedom."

"*No* is the most beautiful word in the English language."

It's wildly interesting that it took me half a century of life to realize these things. I literally lived my life with the purpose of pleasing other people with little to no boundaries and having such a difficult time saying *no*. Mind you, saying *no* still doesn't come easily for me. After forty years of struggling with it, I still hesitate and worry the other person will be upset.

Rachel went on to say, "Boundaries allow us to make our decisions and to live within the freedom of a balanced life. Boundaries are the key to everything. And we as women especially grow up saying *yes* to everything when we should say *no* to so many things. We are taught to be people pleasers, be friendly, don't hurt people's feelings, and don't offend anyone. And then what happens is we have no control. We have no plan. We have no goal, and we find ourselves thirty years old, divorced with kids, and wondering how this even happened. We're not driving the bus. We're just on the bus."

Well, that pretty much described what my life looked like at thirty in a nutshell. All the women in my family were people pleasers, not arguing or standing up for themselves but, instead, trying to make everyone happy while just making themselves miserable. When I left my husband, I still sought out male attention and long relationships with my main goal being to bend over backward to please my partner no matter what. It's much more common for women to be people pleasers than men, partly because of the societal expectations I discussed earlier.

This whole topic came up again when I embarked on a journey to expand my self-confidence in the field of animal communication. After I had my breakthrough in my relationships with Jack, I realized I really am very in tune with what animals are trying to tell us. I just wasn't confident enough to trust myself. I embarked on a journey of psychic development with a wonderful local metaphysical tea shop called The Healing Brew.

As a young child, I was extremely intuitive. I always knew who was calling on the other end of the phone. Yes, I am so old we had no caller ID back then. I used to play with the Ouija board by myself and *loved* seances, astrology, and psychics. I was elated when I stumbled upon this wonderful little shop while attending a course about herbs. The class really forces students to trust themselves, believe in what they are thinking, and be brave enough to share it with others.

I also had the pleasure of interviewing Reverend Bryan Peters and Reverend Steph Allison from The Healing Brew. Bryan is an intuitive herbalist who has extensive knowledge from his grandmother of traditional and folk medicinal skills from the mountains of Appalachia and the Crow nation. He is a psychic medium, reiki master, and has many other healing certifications.

Steph's intuitive abilities enable her to connect with guides, angels, and power animals to assist in the synchronicities that connect us all to bring clarity, focus, and insights on our Earth walk. Steph is involved in assisting others in developing their own intuitive and psychic abilities through classes at The Healing Brew. We discussed the role and expectations of women in society, confidence, and how fear plays such a strong role in people's lives. Bryan put it simply when he said, "What is a confident women called?"

I said the first thing that came to my mind… "A bitch?"

"You're exactly right," he said. "And what about a confident man?"

"Strong and successful," I said.

The sad fact is that this viewpoint has put women in a place where they are basically afraid to stand up for themselves. Both The Healing Brew and Whitehawk Ranch have a mentality that to be able to get past the fear, which is really what holds people back, you must face that fear head on.

As Rachel put it, "Be comfortable in the uncomfortable." She achieves this through work with horses. "The minute you go to your horse, you better be on because your relationship with this horse is defined by the boundaries you set for him or her since that's what they need. It's the only way to be safe and really enjoy these animals. They're flight animals, not predators. So they need us to create those boundaries." Simply put, boundaries keep us safe. They protect us from doing things that may be harmful to us mentally, physically, and emotionally. They also help ensure we attract the right people and situations by sticking to our values and being our true selves.

I also discussed this when chatting with Bryan and Steph at The Healing Brew. Bryan says they find many people living in that fear, and that's what hold them back from "trusting themselves, having confidence in themselves, and making a true intuitive decision." Fear is a huge point of discussion and thing to overcome in their psychic development classes. The classes help people tune in to their psychic abilities and learn to trust what their gut is telling them. People come lacking confidence and not being able to trust their own intuition.

Just as Rachel does with the women at Whitehawk Ranch, The Healing Brew does with their students… make them comfortable being uncomfortable. Students go through many exercises where they must stand up and say what they are thinking about a person, a card, or a thought that comes to their mind. Then they must read oracle cards for each other.

I thought, *I can't do this. I don't know what I am doing.* I had a total lack of confidence and thought everyone would be better at this than I was, just like I have thought about past jobs, horse riding, etc. But guess what? I trusted myself, let go of my fear, and the things I said were all spot on! Bryan and Steph both shared that many times people come in labeling themselves a certain way and believing they are unable to change. As Bryan said, "If you label yourself a victim, you will be a victim."

With Rachel, I had a similar discussion about people labeling themselves. Rachel tells them: "Let's assume for the sake of argument and the sake of this course, that you have developed a way of coping that is very personal to you and very habit forming to you. But let's try to change those habits and see what happens in six months."

She says it's life-changing for all of the women she works with. She also says it's important to address what goes along with boundaries, which is helping people decide what they want in their life, what kind of behavior they are willing to tolerate, and what behavior, quite frankly, they are not. And let's face it, if you can stand up to a big powerful horse, you can stand up to people.

Steph and I spoke a lot about societal expectations and how that can impact people's confidence. When we look at culture, religion and social media, a lot of rules and expectations can cause self-sabotage or cause people to think they aren't good enough or need to fit into what society expects.

Steph said, "People need to learn it's okay to say *no*. It's okay to share your feelings. It's okay to release people who just aren't good for your life, and it's okay to let good things into your life. In relationships, many people are afraid to let go and end relationships because they don't have the confidence that they can make it on their own."

People limit themselves due to lack of confidence and put themselves into a box. Let's consider the professional athlete. According to an article published by Trine University, "Athletes that allow the smallest amount of self-doubt into their thinking will most likely see a decrease in their performance. Self-confidence can make or break an athlete's performance because it facilitates concentration, affects goals, increases effort, and more."[1]

I was married to a professional hockey player for nine years and dated him for three years prior. I also have a son who was a Division 1 kicker in college. It's hard to find more confidence than what you see in a professional athlete. Sometimes they even come off as arrogant. But they trust themselves one hundred percent. They have to because if they hesitate at the wrong moment or doubt creeps in, guess what… they lose!

I can tell you from experience that the professional athlete loses at *nothing*! My ex-husband and I played every single physical and mental game you can think of, and he *always* won! He played tennis against me with his left hand… he won. We played checkers… he won. One day it was raining and we played at least one hundred games of Euchre. *He won them all!*

He was a small center forward when he played hockey, and he was the top scorer on every team he played for. Sometimes he was called a puck hog. But guess what? He *knew* he would make the shot and score the goal. He never doubted himself, never hesitated. He made almost every penalty shot he took. And that is not all skill. That is confidence and believing in yourself.

My son *always* chose the position that in my eyes was the most stressful. He was a goalie when he played soccer, a pitcher when he played baseball, and then a kicker when he played football. As a kicker, focus is the number one most important thing. Controlling your mind, knowing you will make that goal, visualizing the ball going between the posts and completely erasing any previous miss. Total confidence in yourself and your abilities is crucial.

Athletes win because they are confident, they trust themselves, and they don't give up. I played sports when I was young, but I was never the best in any team sports. I always felt others were better. When I played soccer, I would pass the ball more than shoot because I didn't have the confidence that I would score. Track was different. I knew I could run fast, and I was highly competitive, resulting in me being very successful.

When I rode my horse competitively, he taught me that I needed to be confident that I wanted to go over that jump, or he wasn't going! When I jumped regularly, on my way to ride, I would visualize us going over the jumps and doing wonderfully, and we would. But if I went out feeling a bit nervous about it and not really wanting to jump, it was a mess! Another great example of how horses teach us about ourselves and teach us to be confident. Jack taught me all of the above... trust myself, be confident, and don't give up.

It's funny that in my professional life with clients I always had that confidence and the boundaries. Maybe because it's not such a personal relationship, and I am not necessarily craving acceptance but rather wanting to win the deal. Sales is a great example of how people will follow confident people. If someone is trying to sell you anything at all, and they are confident in the value it brings and what it's worth, you will likely buy it. But if they agree with things you may not like about it or lower its price and don't appear confident, well why would you buy it? Life is really no different.

We can all be confident winners. We can all set boundaries and be free to live and enjoy our lives and be happy. Breaking yourself out of a preconceived, long-held view of yourself is *not* easy. If you have been a people pleaser or fixer all your life, saying *no* is *damn* hard. Setting boundaries is *damn* hard too. But if you don't break out of your comfort zone, you will never be able to fix yourself and break out of the mold you may have been put into by yourself, your family, or your friends to find your true potential.

CHAPTER 15

Human Animal Connection

"Until one has loved an animal, a part of one's soul remains unawakened."

—ANATOLE FRANCE

Just about anyone who has had a pet is very aware of the unconditional love, joy, and understanding an animal can bring to your life. I am not sure, however, how aware most humans are of the intense energy connection that goes on between animals and humans as well as animals and animals.

I have become intimately aware of how sensitive animals are to energy in the last seven years practicing animal massage. I truly love the animals. I am there to help them, and they sense that. Many owners tell me their animal doesn't like to be touched, is afraid of people, and the list goes on.

Once I begin my session, I consistently hear things like, "Oh my gosh, he doesn't do that with anyone."

I have dogs kiss me that don't even kiss their owners, and horses melt like butter to my touch when the owner can't go near the area. Why is that? An animal can sense if you are nervous or worried something is going to happen, and quite honestly, if you think they are going to elicit a certain behavior, they most likely will.

I mentioned in an earlier chapter about riding a horse that spooked at the woods and dumped everyone. But he didn't dump me. Why? Probably because I didn't expect that he would, and I didn't worry or even think about it. When I first begin to massage dogs, nine times out of ten they are excited for a few minutes because I am a new person petting them, and then they get worried.

They think, *Why are you petting me that way? Are you the vet? Am I getting a shot? Who are you?* But slowly they realize from my touch and my emotions that I am there to help them feel better, that my touch is healing, and within thirty minutes most of them are snoozing.

Horses are *much* more expressive and sometimes react to pressure as light as you would put on a raw egg when not wanting to break the yolk. At first they may have wide worried eyes and tense, stressed energy just from their lives. Soon, their eyes get sleepy, they start licking and chewing and yawning, and their lips droop and quiver. All of these are signs of release and relaxation. Sometimes I need to tell the owners to go away or let me hold their lead rope because many times the owners are unknowingly full of nervous energy, which they are passing on to their horse.

Being flight animals and animals of prey, horses are very in tune with their surroundings and the energy and body language of their herd or people around them. According to an article in *Jumper Nation*, "Horses have incredible hearing, with the ability to hear the heartbeat of a human from four feet away. In the wild, horses will synchronize their heartbeats to the other horses in the herd in order to sense danger more quickly, and recent studies have shown that they use those tactics in domesticated life as well. When our horses interact with us, they tend to synchronize to our heartbeats as well, meaning they can sense slight adjustments in our mood. This means when us riders get nervous about something, we inadvertently translate our fears and anxieties onto our horses."[1]

A horse will reflect back everything a human is sending their way because of these sensitivities. This requires a different relationship than a human would have with a dog. People commonly make that mistake in a relationship with a horse, as I did at first with Jack.

"They fail to establish leadership within the relationship… The horse is a herd animal, and within the herd, there has to be a hierarchy and a leader responsible for everyone's safety. Horses demand this. Being a herd animal isn't something the horse chooses; it's how he's made."[2]

When speaking with Rachel Whitehawk, I also learned more about her clients. "I have girls who sometimes come from the penal system, sometimes juvenile hall, sometimes homeless shelters. They come from all different places… Human trafficking, I'll talk about the need for new boundaries," said Rachel.

Rachel said many of the women are terrified, having a hard time sitting in the uncomfortable, and a hard time regulating their emotions. As a result they are unable to make decisions based on some logic rather than pure emotion. She has horses trained to specifically *not* move when these women illicit a fear response, which is actually opposite to their instincts. As a result, it takes a certain horse to be a part of this program. This allows the women to persist, stay, build confidence, calm down and "get comfortable with the uncomfortable."

She goes on to say, "Horses can help us learn to regulate internally. Because if we don't, we really can't be safe with them. They will never respect or trust us. And I honestly believe that without trust and without respect with horses, you've got no relationship, but I think the same thing exists in in human relationships. Because it is so hard to have a relationship with a man if there's no respect. He could appreciate you, and he could enjoy your company. But if he doesn't respect who you are and what you stand for, you're not getting the type of relationship you deserve.

"Horses also force you to be honest with yourself and get in touch with your emotions. When we immediately react out of anger or fear, and fear is the number one motivator in our lives, we set in motion a disconnect in the relationship with a horse. It's the same thing with people. When women make emotionally charged decisions with people, they will not get the outcome they are hoping for."

Rachel has practiced this philosophy with horses and humans most of her life. She is Native American in heritage and learned horsemanship from her father, a Native American horse trainer. Their philosophy is not about dominance or force but about leadership and trust. She explained that the tribal communities had no fencing to confine the horses like we do. But the horses chose to stay within the tribal community because that is where they found protection and safety because of the trust that they had built with the humans.

I learned how well this philosophy works with horses when I began practicing the techniques of Carson James, who is really a hero in my life. I also was lucky enough to be able to interview him. His training techniques allowed me to transform my relationship with Jack.

When I asked him what horses had taught him in life, he said, "Humility, empathy, communication skills, simplicity, forgiveness, perseverance, awareness, consistency, focus, positivity, time-management." How amazing is that? He also said working with horses really changed the way he interacted with people because: "Working with horses forces you to get to the root of an issue, so you find yourself doing the same with people. Instead of taking a behavior at face value, you try to see the underlying cause."

You cannot go into a working session with a horse and expect to follow your agenda and your timeline. You cannot be in a hurry or in an angry mood. And if you are, the horse will reflect that right back at you. The horse also forces you to be very particular with your asks as well as persistent. A horse cannot plan to be mischievous or bad. A horse will do what's easy. If he doesn't do what you ask, you likely aren't asking in a way so he understands it's best for him. He is going to do what's best for his survival.

Carson goes on to say: "A horse is the most moldable creature on earth. It's almost never the horse's fault. For example, I once had someone say their horse would not let them spray him with a water hose. They were convinced the horse was deathly afraid of water. But when it rains outside, the horse calmly grazes in the pasture as the raindrops pour down on him. So the water is not the problem. It's the way the human is exposing the horse to the water. The approach is wrong. We need to stop blaming the horse and realize that everything a horse does, good or bad, is *the result of how a human interacted with that horse.*"

A horse really forces you to slow down and think about how you are asking, how you are presenting, and what you are expecting in return. The horse learns from release. Be very specific with what you are asking. Don't ask something the horse cannot yet understand. Break it down into small bites. And when the horse gets the right answer, immediately stop asking. The release is his reward and the way he knows he did the right thing. It's fairly simple. I am 99 percent sure if we took the time to do this in our human relationships, we would likely also get much better outcomes.

I worked with another amazing horse trainer who came to visit Jack and me during my time of desperation. Adam Black of Adam Black Horsemanship pushed me over the hump to gain the confidence I needed.

He said, "We need to step back and think about the fact that they're a prey animal and we, as a predator, strap a dead piece of animal, meaning a saddle, on them and confine them and say, 'Don't worry. It's all okay.' I think if a lot of people start to think about this when they think about how to approach a horse to where it makes sense to them, things would get along so much easier and quicker."

The owner at Forever Amber Acres Animal Sanctuary learned quickly how sensitive horses react to people's emotions and thoughts. Forever Amber Acres Animal Sanctuary provides safe refuge, purposeful rehabilitation, and retirement aftercare for special needs horses and other animals to serve military veterans, children, families, and seniors dealing with physical and emotional challenges.

I spoke with their founder Michele Bolinger about how she sees horses impacting people's lives in her program. Michele says many times people enter a session trying to put on a front and not sharing their real truths, but the horses force them to be their real selves. It's magical how the horses work.

A good example was a client who came to a session saying everything was okay, happy-go-lucky. The horses created a barrier between him and the treatment team as if to say, *This guy has a wall up around him.* Slow but surely, he put down his wall and the horses moved away. She says these types of things happen regularly where the horses mirror the person's mood or behavior and force them to get real with themselves and the treatment team.

Michele was a victim of domestic violence. Through her work with these special needs horses, she has transformed into someone completely different. She says she doesn't even recognize who she used to be. Horses helped her become the confident person who would never take any of the abuse she did in past. With these special needs horses, you cannot afford to show fear or doubt or lack of confidence. They come from such traumatic pasts, and they will sense that weakness and fear and act out. They have helped change her life.

When you consider all these things we should consider in building relationships with horses, is it really much different with people? People want to be understood. People don't want to be forced to do things they don't understand. People want to do what's best for their survival and happiness and to be with someone who's going to make that possible.

People want to be with someone they trust, who won't hurt them and is confident and strong. But if you just say *yes* all the time to what someone wants, that doesn't provide them with any direction or leadership or sense of confidence from you that they need to be able to feel safe in the relationship. It was the same with Jack, and the transformation occurred once I had the confidence in myself.

The difference is people *can* plot to be mischievous, hurtful, and evil. People can make you doubt yourself and who you are by being deceitful. Animals cannot lie and cannot make you believe you are anything other than what you are putting out there. They will let you know the energy you are reflecting and how you can become your best self if you just take the time to listen.

CHAPTER 16:

Love Yourself and Love Unconditionally

———

One thing I have learned for certain through all the relationships that have been sent my way is that in order to love someone else and have a healthy relationship, you must first love yourself… unconditionally. You must learn to be happy with yourself. You must learn to be happy alone.

If you rely on someone else to bring or create your happiness, you will never be happy. And guess what? Neither will they! It took me over forty years to be perfectly happy alone and not in a relationship. Before then I was more or less in a serious relationship or in a series of fun, less serious relationships. But I *always* had a man of some sort in my life.

It's painfully difficult to be alone at first. It's quiet. It's lonely. And it's unusual. I did a lot of crying, a lot of being mad at myself, feeling sorry for myself, and boy did I put up *a lot* of walls. Some of those walls are still there and may never come down. Hurt and betrayal do that sometimes. But I have learned what I want for myself, what's important to me, and what I won't sacrifice for myself and my happiness. As a result, I will be a better partner.

I have learned to love myself, the good and the bad. And I have learned to love my life so much. Because my life is now *my life*. Many people tell me I am the most positive person they know. As I said earlier in the book, where attention goes, energy flows! I believe you should always put positive energy out there to manifest what you desire.

I have never made it a point to think negatively or get down and depressed about things that go wrong. But past relationships and trying to always make someone else happy, always trying to love unconditionally, does cause some internal stress. Now I am pursuing *my* passions, not someone else's. I am doing things to make myself happy, not someone else. And in return, I am a happier, more giving, and more loving person to my friends and family.

My actions and plans used to be guided by thoughts of, *Will my partner like this? Will he think I look nice? Will it make him happy?* Now I don't need to give any of that a second thought. I don't have to wash my hair for five days and worry about if it smells. And, really, my partner should love my smelly hair and all, but I would have never thought that way!

Funnily enough, though, I have always been that way with my partners. When I am in love, I am in love *unconditionally*—smelly hair and all. I always said, "I don't get mad unless it's a sin." And I pretty much stood by that. I even let sins slide. In fact, I let almost everything slide.

I made my best effort to understand my partners' thoughts and actions based on how they were brought up and how they may have seen things from their point of view. I would let my point of view and values fall by the wayside.

I 100 percent believe that love should be unconditional. People make mistakes. People aren't perfect, and you should never expect something in return for your own good deeds. However, people can be hurtful and disrespectful, and that is when the unconditional love for yourself needs to stand strong. You may still love that person, but you need to be able to take yourself out of situations and relationships that are hurtful. It is definitely a hard act to balance.

With a disrespectful horse, expectations and communications need to be very black and white… very easy to understand. I love my horse unconditionally. Period. He could trample me, but I would still love him. Now, let's keep in mind, that a horse has no ability to plan to be bad or evil or anything of the sort.

A horse will do what is made easy, and what will keep him alive. He also will strive to be a leader. In every interaction with a horse, he determines if you are a leader or if he is the leader. It takes only one time for you to make a wrong move, and he determines he is the leader. Here is the best example of loving my horse but setting my boundary.

My horse has his halter on and a lead rope attached. I ask him to stand. That means he does not take one step unless I say. It is much like asking a dog to stay. However, in the mind of a horse, the one who moves the other's feet is in charge. For example, when you watch horses in the pasture, the leader always pushes the others around and makes them move their feet to another part of the pasture.

I ask him to walk to the right, and the left, and I am in charge. If he chooses to walk toward me, and I step back one step, now he is in charge. In this scenario, I have asked him to stand. I walk away, and he must stand still. Now, in the past, if he stood a few minutes and then decided he wanted to come to see me, I would have thought *Aw, he loves me... how cute* and give him a pet.

That's the wrong idea because now he moved toward me without me asking and took a leadership stance. We all crave attention and for someone to love us, so it sounds nice. *Wrong.* The horse just decided by himself to walk over to me, which to him translates into him being the leader.

Now, in the new world where I am confident and love myself first, my horse takes one step toward me, and I immediately tell him to back up three steps and now stand. And guess what? Now he knows who is in charge. He isn't mad at me. He doesn't love someone else more who lets him walk over to them and pet him. He isn't going to walk away and not want to come see me next time I visit. In fact, he respects me more and wants to be around me more. And I still unconditionally love him. But I set a boundary to protect myself because I love myself unconditionally too.

I am superb at unconditional love. I did a numerology class and my read-out was filled with more eights than any number. Too much of something is not a good thing either, and of course, eight is all about unconditional love.

Just like the therapist said to me long ago, "Jill, it's great that you see the good in everyone and love them despite their faults, but you are failing to see the red flags that are hurting you and running right by them!" The big thing I was missing was the self-love.

Mayim Bialik stated in one of her podcasts: "When you love yourself enough, meaning when you understand your needs enough and believe that they are worthy, you will no longer find attractive people who cannot fulfill those things for you."[1]

Before I had learned to love myself and love being alone, and before I had learned my lessons from Jack, I could never have been the partner I am today. Now I can be more honest, not worrying about hurting my partners' feelings or about them walking away. Now I can be happy being alone when my partner wants to do things with friends or have time alone or whatever it may be because I am not worrying their request is about me and my shortcomings. Now I can make decisions that will also be in my best interest, making me a happier person to be around. And now I can confidently set boundaries, which people actually crave. Nobody wants to be with a wallowing ninny who can't make a decision or be confident in their likes and choices.

I have also learned that expectations lead to disappointment. You can only control and change yourself. And I promise, when you love yourself and let life happen, your life will become a fairytale when you least expect it. So love your partner, your horse, your friends, your animals, your family, and your children so unconditionally that both yours and their hearts burst with joy.

But most importantly... *love yourself the most.*

CHAPTER 17

The World Is Your Oyster—Love Yourself, Love Your Life

"One of the greatest regrets in life is being what others would want you to be, rather than being yourself."
—SHANNON L. ALDER

Everyone is born onto this planet Earth as a little helpless baby. Not one baby is better than the other baby. They are all equal and all reliant on the world and people around them to help them grow, understand, and survive. Unfortunately, all babies are not born into equally supportive families and situations, and this is where self-doubt and struggles can begin.

It took me over half a century to really accept myself, love myself for who I am, and love the life I have created. Until then, I fumbled along through life at one hundred miles an hour, always thinking everyone else must know more than I did and be better than I was and likely didn't look up to me for my knowledge and expertise. Why in the world would that be true?

I have always been at the top of my class in most things I try, have won lots of blue ribbons riding horses, have managed to earn a great living selling people a variety of things, and helped a huge number of animals live less stressful, more pain-free lives. But despite all that, I would never have thought I knew better than someone else. And I strongly believe you should never stop learning because some people *always* know things you may not know, and you always have things you can learn. But that doesn't mean anyone is necessarily *better* or that you are inferior.

The lessons my horse Jack has taught me in setting boundaries and self-confidence have changed just about every aspect of my life. For the first time, I interviewed as one hundred percent myself and have a job where I am respected for exactly who I am and valued for my years of sales experience and knowledge. Although I can no longer ride my own horse, I now realize I have an enormous amount of knowledge not only about riding horses but about all areas of communicating and interacting with them. Because of this, I am now confident enough to ride other people's horses.

I choose the people I want to spend time with and no longer give in to doing things that I really don't have time for in my schedule. I also choose to spend time with just myself and my animals because I realize my alone time is peaceful, therapeutic, and necessary. I help my dad since my mom has passed but not to the extent of sacrificing my professional life, my personal life, or my health. I don't bother wasting efforts to communicate with family members who have never supported me or even reached out to me, and I don't feel bad about it.

I am definitely better at setting boundaries and expressing what is not acceptable. A colleague I used to work with came to town recently and wanted to have dinner. We traveled together extensively, became good friends, and stayed in touch. *Just* friends always, nothing else even crossed my mind, and I didn't think it had crossed his, as after all, he was married.

He met me at my barn. I tried to take a picture of us to put on Facebook for our old colleagues, and he highly objected, which I found odd. That evening, we went out to eat and talked about old times and people we knew. We had a blast. At one point he put his hand on my leg, which was uncomfortable, but I just brushed it off. When we left and were saying bye, he tried to kiss me.

Now, in the past, I would have maybe brushed it off, quickly said bye, and that would be that. I would have been horrified. Well, new me said, "What the hell are you doing? No wonder you don't want me to put your picture on Facebook! You are married. What the hell?"

He proceeded to tell me he would be leaving his wife one day. The relationship had fizzled and he always liked me and on and on. I told him this was all ridiculous. He needed to get a grip and have a nice night! *Men!* In the past I probably would have been flattered and somewhat let it slide to not hurt his feelings.

I also nearly made a very poor decision regarding someone I thought was a super nice guy. I met him about seven years into my relationship hiatus. He gave me a bit of a "poor me" story, which I totally fell for, of course wanting to fix people and see the good things in them. We were friends and had a bit of sexual tension. Luckily with my newfound confidence and ability to set boundaries, I took a step back and learned that may have been one of the worst choices I could have ever made. So, yes, I am slowly trusting my instincts after over forty years of poor decisions.

Keep in mind, my instincts were always there. I just allowed myself to not listen to them and to be manipulated and sucked into trying to fix everyone. One thing I will *never* do is internet dating. Instincts can't work very well over a computer screen. I can't come to terms with any of that. I still feel a need for in-person chemistry and a real sense of that true person. If I made bad decisions with the real person, I can't imagine how snowed I would be by fabulous internet profiles!

As for the million-dollar question you are all likely asking about…men…well… I am getting there. After almost ten years of being single, I definitely have learned to stand up for myself and maybe consider some kind of relationship… *Maybe!*

Am I in a relationship now? That's complicated because, if I have realized one thing for certain, it's that the universe will never send me simple. Maybe it's because I am strong enough for complicated? Someone has re-entered my life recently from way back in the day.

I was on a job interview one morning in April of 2023, eating breakfast at a local restaurant I rarely visit. A guy walked up to my booth, longish hair, beard… kinda hot and messy, which is my thing.

He said, "I hate to bother you. I hate to interrupt and be that guy, but are you Jill?"

I think I looked at him cross-eyed thinking, *Who the hell are you?* I said, "Yes, who are you?"

As soon as those words rolled off my tongue it hit me like a ton of bricks!

I was trying to say his name, but I just squealed and screamed, giving him a big hug and making a total scene at the restaurant and on this interview. Remember the singer who asked if he could kiss me? *Twenty-five* years have passed and he recognized me? I haven't seen or heard from him in *all* this time. I did think about him from time to time, and oddly enough I had thought of that band a couple weeks prior. That is how the world works… Where attention goes, energy flows. Anyway, we exchanged numbers. I told him to let me know when he had a gig, and I would go watch him sing.

I kept thinking about him, which was annoying because I haven't thought about a guy in years, which makes life easy, stress-free, and heart-break free. This was such a crazy twist of fate after all these years, and I couldn't help but think there must be a big reason for this.

He texted a couple of weeks later, and we finally chatted. I found out he is a grandpa. This was such an *extreme* time warp because to me, he is twenty-five years old. I learned that he lives five minutes from my house. And I have never run into him in twenty-five years? He even lived right up the road from me for a while. *Crazy!* It's like some kind of divine intervention.

We have talked and texted a lot. I went to watch him sing. We went to lunch, and he bought my lunch. Um… I am not sure anyone I have dated in the last quarter of a century has bought me anything… not that I care but the point is worth noting. I met him recently at a bar and dragged a good friend along and to the gig because, remember, from here on out, any man I may have interest in needs to be screened like ten times over.

We were sitting at the bar and he said, "Can I kiss you?"

Well… c'mon! Déjà vu… um… of course! A little PDA never hurt anyone. Right? He is a crazy good kisser, and we made out in his truck like high school kids. So… now what? It's a slow road for sure. Oddly enough, it usually takes sex to really get me hooked, but we aren't there yet. This is much different. He makes me laugh and smile every time I talk to him or see him. We are having a lot of fun. I am guarded. He is guarded.

Recently I said to him, "But I think you are a bit scared of me?"

"I'm not scared of anything," he said. "I am cautious. Cautious to not hurt you."

Well cautious is putting it mildly for me. And this also must mean something could hurt me. Regardless, this touched my heart. No man has ever been this honest and upfront with me nor seemed to care much about hurting me. It's all new ground. I'm scared. I'm nervous. And, yeah, I like him… *a lot*. And yeah, I think he is a good guy, but I am trying to look out for red flags, still have my wall up, and am allowing my friends to help guide me.

I'm not sure I trust them more than I trust myself at this point, but in the past, they were always right while I was always wrong. Most importantly, this relationship is full of honesty, trust, and communication, which is what I need most based on my past experiences. And, yes, it is testing my boundaries. Regardless, it will be a slow, careful journey.

Yes, I am getting there. We shall see where life takes us.

I am definitely not totally fixed yet. Who knows if I ever will be… but that isn't the point. The point is growth, being confident, and loving yourself.

An old friend recently said to me, "You are the happiest person I know."

That filled my heart with joy. Because I am truly happy! And as you have read, it's been a journey.

Find a way to understand your true self and the energy you are reflecting and trust your intuition. Hopefully, by sharing my journey, I can help you find the courage and confidence to love yourself, be yourself, and fix yourself in order to live the life you have always dreamed of. After all, we only have one life. *Live, love, and be happy!*

Acknowledgments

To all of my family, friends and relationships past and present, I want to extend my most heartfelt thanks. Without all of you in my life, this book would never have been a concept. Whether you provided lessons to me along the way in my life or support during this writing process and throughout my life, I absolutely would not be here without you.

The journey of writing this book has been a truly amazing one! Above all, I thank the universe for putting my horse Jack into my life. He has inspired so much change in my life, was the catalyst for writing this book, and is a true part of my soul. I also thank the universe for showing me I could open my heart to love again, love myself at the same time, and continue to learn lessons that make me wiser and stronger.

I would also like to thank all of you who took the time to chat with me and whose stories I share in this book. Dr. William Bixler, Brenda Hanson, Michele Bolinger, Adam Black, Carson James, Rachel Whitehawk, Bryan Peters, and Steph Allison… your input was invaluable!

You all have been such an inspiration to me throughout my journey. Horse trainers Carson James and Adam Black, you are my heroes! The transformation I had with my horse would never have been possible without your guidance and support.

I am extremely grateful for Misty Acres of Bath, Forever Amber Acres Animal Sanctuary, The Healing Brew, Whitehawk Ranch, and Yoga Bliss, who have offered to host launch events and provided event packages to support my presale campaign. And I am so blessed to have the most amazing photographer the universe has to offer, my friend Matt Platz. The emotion and connection between Jack and me that is captured in your work is breathtaking!

A huge thank you to the Manuscripts team who provided such amazing support and direction. Without all of them, this would not have been possible. A special call out to my editors Angela Mitchell and Chrissy Wolfe, who kept me believing in myself and provided constant encouragement and laughs along the way.

This book was made possible also by a community of people who so strongly believed in me that they preordered their copies and helped promote the book before it even went to print. Thanks to you all, many of whom read my early manuscript and gave input on the book title and cover. You are amazing, and I am so grateful for all of you. As promised, you are in the book (listed in alphabetical order by first name):

Abbey and Kevin Maltz	Anthony Viola
Adrienne Six	Arlene Cowan
Angela Ramos	Belinda Carroll

Beverly Craggs
Brian Aberth
Brook Jenkins
Carey Cameron-Davis
Carole Pensom
Catherine Slocom
Catie Schnell
Chris Rogers
Christina Carter
Christine Lantzer
Cindy Wise
Courtney Farr
Danielle Shields
David Walter
David Ricketts
David Thompson
Debbie Jones
Diana Ward
Diane Liddle
Domenico Barbaro
Donna Warner
Dylan Rosenberg
Elora Luke
Eric Johnson
Eric Revesz
Geri Atwood
Heather Welborn
Ian Pensom
Jane Cameron
Janel Filips
Jennifer DeTracy
Jill Nielsen

Jim Brungo
Jo-Ellen Burke
John Blackfan
Justin Janczewski
Karen Feetterers
Karen Soini
Karen Priemer
Katherine Judge
Kathy Corrado
Katie Dubois
Krisann and Pete Lucrezi
Kristen Campbell
Laura Adams
Leslie Armour
Lesley Carr
Leslie Vaughn
Linda Manfull
Lisa Martino-Cugini
Lisa Kleines
Lois Netta
Lu Semenzin
Marc Stringer
Marty Dunne
Mary Getz
Matthew Platz
Melanie Flowers
Michael Simon
Michael Weinberger
Michele Bolinger
Molly Zoeller
Nannette Mitchell
Nerijus Steponavicius

Pamela Guerin
Patricia Klein
Paul Barriga
Phyllis Vair
Rachel Ruffer
Rachel Elend
Rob Ewing
Robert Cadenhead
Sabrina Sawan
Sean Lasher
Sharon Anderson
Shirley Keller

Stacy Draffan
Susan Swan
Susie Kleines
Suzan Edwards
Tamie and Kurt Fennell
Thomas Dye
Tina Wetmore
Tracy Murphy-Tibbits
Tracy Appel
Yada Sok
Yolanda McGuinness
Yonit Kraushar

Notes

CHAPTER 1: HORSES ARE THE BEST TEACHERS

1. PonyMomAmmy, "Sometimes It Seems That the Biggest Lessons Horses Teach Us Have Nothing to Do with Riding," *Featured* (blog), *The Plaid Horse,* January 14, 2020, https://www.theplaidhorse.com/2020/01/14/sometimes-it-seems-that-the-biggest-lessons-horses-teach-us-have-nothing-to-do-with-riding/amp/.
2. Ibid.
3. PonyMomAmmy, "Sometimes It Seems the Biggest Lessons Horses Teach Us Have Nothing to Do with Riding," *Featured* (blog), *The Plaid Horse,* January 14, 2020, https://www.theplaidhorse.com/2020/01/14/sometimes-it-seems-that-the-biggest-lessons-horses-teach-us-have-nothing-to-do-with-riding/amp/.

CHAPTER 4: PARENTS... OH PARENTS... AND FAMILY... OH FAMILY!

1. Ryan Light, "Fatherless Daughter Syndrome: The Effects of an Absent Father on a Girl," *Blog* (blog), *Beat Anxiety*, May 1,

2023, https://beatanxiety.me/fatherless-daughter-syndrome-psychological-effects-of-an-absent-father-on-a-girl/.

CHAPTER 5: LET'S TALK ABOUT SEX, BABY

1. Katie Haller, "The Truth behind Why Women Find It Harder to Have Casual Sex than Men," *Lifestyle* (blog), *The Elite Daily*, April 18, 2014, https://www.elitedaily.com/women/oxytocin-science-makes-harder-women-casual-sex.
2. Ibid.
3. Katie Haller, "The Truth Behind Why Women Find It Harder to Have Casual Sex Than Men," *Lifestyle* (blog), *The Elite Daily*, April 18, 2014, https://www.elitedaily.com/women/oxytocin-science-makes-harder-women-casual-sex.

CHAPTER 6: MEN, MEN…

1. Ryan Light, "Fatherless Daughter Syndrome: The Effects of an Absent Father on a Girl," *Blog* (blog), *Beat Anxiety*, May 1, 2023, https://beatanxiety.me/fatherless-daughter-syndrome-psychological-effects-of-an-absent-father-on-a-girl/.

CHAPTER 8: ALONG CAME A SEX ADDICT

1. Cleveland Clinic, "Sex Addiction, Hypersexuality and Compulsive Sexual Behavior," *Diseases and Conditions* (blog), *Cleveland Clinic*, April 5, 2022, https://my.clevelandclinic.org/health/diseases/22690-sex-addiction-hypersexuality-and-compulsive-sexual-behavior.

CHAPTER 9: ABUSIVE RELATIONSHIPS

1. Christine Louis de Canonville, "Home," Narcissistic Behavior, March 1, 2023, https://narcissisticbehavior.net.
2. Kaytee Gillis, "16 Signs of Narcissistic Abuse and Victim Syndrome," *Relationships* (blog), *Choosing Therapy*, June 14,

2023, https://www.choosingtherapy.com/narcissistic-abuse-syndrome.

CHAPTER 13: WORKPLACE BOUNDARIES

1. Leo Buscaglia, *Living, Loving, and Learning* (New York, NY: Ballantine Books, 1983), 58.

CHAPTER 14: CONFIDENCE AND BOUNDARIES

1. Center for Sports Studies "The Relationship between Self-Confidence and Performance," *Center for Sports Studies* (blog), Trine University, accessed November 3, 2023, https://www.trine.edu/academics/centers/center-for-sports-studies/blog/2023/the_relationship_between_self-confidence_and_performance.aspx.

CHAPTER 15: HUMAN ANIMAL CONNECTION

1. Leslie Wylie, "Two Bodies, One Heart: Horses and Your Heartbeat," *Barn Aisle* (blog), *Jumper Nation,* December 16, 2020, https://jumpernation.com/two-bodies-one-heart-horses-and-your-heartbeat/.
2. Cynthia McFarland, "How to Speak Horse," *Horse Care* (blog), *Horse Illustrated,* May 24, 2012, https://www.horseillustrated.com/horse-keeping-how-to-speak-horse.

CHAPTER 16: LOVE YOURSELF AND LOVE UNCONDITIONALLY

1. Mayim Bialik, "Dr. David Richo: Don't Bring Childhood Wounds into Adult Relationships," Mayim Bialik's Breakdown, August 22, 2023, 1:30:18, https://www.youtube.com/watch?v=qa9IX9ko8sQ.